The Supreme Court Historical Society

Supreme Court Historical Society

Board of Trustees

General Statement

The Supreme Court Historical Society is a private non-profit organization, incorporated in the District of Columbia in 1974. The Society is dedicated to the collection and preservation of the history of the Supreme Court of the United States.

The Society seeks to accomplish its mission by supporting historical research, collecting antiques and artifacts relating to the Court's history, and publishing books and other materials which increase public awareness of the Court's contribution to our Nation's rich constitutional heritage.

Since 1975, the Society has been publishing a *Quarterly* newsletter, distributed to its membership, which contains short historical pieces on the Court and articles detailing the Society's programs and activities. In 1976, the Society began publishing an annual collection of scholarly articles on the Court's history entitled the *Yearbook,* which was renamed the *Journal of Supreme Court History* in 1990 and became a semi-annual publication in 1996.

The Society initiated the *Documentary History of the Supreme Court of the United States, 1789-1800* in 1977 with a matching grant from the National Historical Publications and Records Commission (NHPRC). The Supreme Court became a cosponsor in 1979. Since that time the Project has completed five of its eight volumes, with Volume 5 published in 1994.

The Society also publishes *Equal Justice Under Law*, a 165-page illustrated history of the Court, in cooperation with the National Geographic Society, the latest edition of which appeared in 1994. In 1986 the Society cosponsored the 300-page *Illustrated History of the Supreme Court of the United States*. It sponsored the publication of the *United States Supreme Court Index to Opinions* in 1981, and funded a ten-year update of that volume in 1994.

In 1993 the Society published, in conjunction with Congressional Quarterly, Inc., *The Supreme Court Justices: Illustrated Biographies, 1789-1993. The Supreme Court Justices,* which has been reedited this year to include the biographies of Justices Ginsburg and Breyer, features numerous rare photographs and other illustrations. It represents a major contribution to the existing works on the Court as it is the first one-volume reference book on the lives of the Justices.

In addition to its research/publications projects, the Society is now cooperating with the Federal Judicial Center on a pilot oral history project on the Supreme Court. The Society is also conducting an active acquisitions program which has contributed substantially to the completion of the Court's permanent collection of busts and portraits, as well as period furnishings, private papers and other artifacts and memorabilia relating to the Court's history. These materials are incorporated into displays prepared by the Court Curator's Office for the benefit of the Court's one million annual visitors.

The Society also funds outside research, awards cash prizes to promote scholarship on the Court and sponsors or cosponsors various lecture series and other educational colloquia to further public understanding of the Court and its history.

The Society ended 1995 with approximately 5,200 members whose financial support and volunteer participation in the Society's standing and ad hoc committees enables the organization to function. These committees report to an elected Board of Trustees and an Executive Committee, the latter of which is principally responsible for policy decisions and for supervising the Society's permanent staff.

Requests for additional information should be directed to the Society's headquarters at 111 Second Street, N.E., Washington, D.C. 20002, Tel. (202) 543-0400.

The Supreme Court and the Civil War

111 Second Street, N.E. Washington, D.C. 20002
ISBN 0-914785-11-7

Introduction: The Supreme Court in the Civil War

Leon Silverman

Mention the Civil War and it conjures up visions of violent clashes between northern and southern armies. Names such as Antietam, Gettysburg, Chickamauga and Cold Harbor are etched in America's collective memory as sites of horrific carnage.

A great number of amateur and professional historians can recount the military campaigns and their associated death tolls in great detail. Ironically, many Civil War buffs are hard-pressed to explain what brought hundreds of thousands of Americans out onto the battlefield.

The Supreme Court in the Civil War traces the origins of the war in constitutional conflicts over slavery and state sovereignty. It examines the Civil War's impact on freedom of speech and the exercise of personal liberties. And, it looks at the precedents established during the war which effectively expanded the President's war powers.

The Supreme Court in the Civil War has its origins in a 1994 lecture series which was organized by the Supreme Court Historical Society and cosponsored by the Friends of the Law Library of Congress. The program included panel discussions and lectures by some of the nation's most respected Civil War and constitutional scholars. Adding to the historic significance of this series, each of the six parts of the program was introduced by a Justice of the Supreme Court, and took place in an historic setting—four in the Supreme Court Chamber, and two in the Great Hall of the Library of Congress.

In reading *The Supreme Court in the Civil War*, the Society's interest in mounting a series on the Civil War becomes apparent immediately. The Civil War was, after all, a constitutional conflict. It was the only time in our history when the Nation was rent by philosophical differences about the government's organization and the limits of its power. Not surprisingly, the Supreme Court played a central role in the constitutional debates over slavery, state sovereignty, the first real application of war powers, and the civil rights questions which followed passage of the three "Reconstruction Amendments."

In an attempt to examine the complex issues which propelled the nation to war, the Society made a concerted effort to approach the topic from diverse perspectives. Among the most hotly debated historical issues arising from the antebellum period, for example, is whether slavery or state sovereignty should be cited as the primary cause of the war—a question which has its roots in the early foundations of the Constitution.

The Constitution recognized slavery, albeit in passing, by adopting a "three-fifths" rule allowing slave-holding states to include slaves in their calculations for purposes of Congressional representation on a three-fifths to one basis. It also set a specific date before which Congress could not terminate the importation of slaves, opening the question of whether the Constitution was a pro-slavery or anti-slavery document. Inclusion of these controversial passages opened a debate whose origins were partly moral, partly economic, and entirely political.

Not surprisingly then, the Society opened the lecture series with a panel discussion entitled "Antebellum Constitutional Crises" which was introduced by Chief Justice William H. Rehnquist. Professor Herman Belz of the University of Maryland at College Park moderated a panel composed of Professors Ludwell Johnson of the College of William and Mary and Larry Kramer of New York University School of Law. The edited text of that, and another panel discussion in the series are both included in this volume. In both cases panelists were selected not only for their expertise, but also because of their divergent views on the issues.

The Supreme Court in the Civil War

"As a constitutional issue, the question of slavery was a relative latecomer," notes panelist Ludwell Johnson in condensing his remarks, "nor was it, as I see it, ever the fundamental issue. . . . At bottom, the question was one of political power." Quoting Jefferson Davis, Professor Johnson characterizes many prewar constitutional battles as "essentially struggles for sectional equality or ascendancy—for the maintenance or destruction of that balance of power or equipoise between North and South which was early recognized as a cardinal principle in our Federal system."

In contrast with the Southern position, Professor Kramer notes, Northerners like Daniel Webster articulated a Nationalist view " . . . that states were subordinate to the federal government in the sense that they had no power to override its actions. The Constitution is a fundamental law of one people, not a compact of states."

Professor Belz, moderated the panel discussion, and observed during the presentation that this debate was not merely an intellectual exercise. Its consequences affected not just the power relationship between the states and the federal government, but the personal freedom of an enslaved race of men and women who, prior to the war, were denied their rights as citizens.

"The Declaration of Independence stated that all men are created equal; it asserted that the equality principle was a self-evident truth," says Belz. "Eleven years later the Constitution recognized the existence of slavery in several of the states. Whether it did more than that was a matter of profound controversy in the period before the Civil War. The disputed points in constitutional law were whether African-Americans were included in the Declaration of Independence, and whether the Constitution was a pro-slavery document which gave affirmative sanction to the institution of Negro servitude, an antislavery document that marked it for ultimate extinction, or a neutral document that took no position on slavery in a substantive sense. The Civil War was fought to resolve these fundamental questions of constitutional law and political philosophy."

Ironically, while constitutional conflicts may have been responsible for bringing the war on, the war spawned additional constitutional crises of its own. For example, in a move to quell the spread of revolt, President Lincoln suspended habeas corpus and authorized the military to arrest thousands of suspected Southern sympathizers, among whom was one John Merryman. These acts brought the President into direct conflict with then Chief Justice Roger B. Taney.

In the second lecture in "The Supreme Court in the Civil War" series University of Kansas Professor Phillip Paludan examined the Taney Court's relationship with the Lincoln Administration during the early years of the war, contrasting Lincoln's and Taney's widely diverging views on slavery's place in the constitution.

"When Taney looked at original intent he saw the constitution as a structure, a system of rules set down in the past which must be followed faithfully by all succeeding generations. But Lincoln had a different view of what it was. He thought that it was a process . . . [which] could respond to new ideas, meet new situations, as well as call people back to contemplate its original ideals and meanings."

Though Taney took firm stands against Lincoln's seeming defiance of the Chief Justice's interpretations of original intent, Taney, and the majority, which produced the *Dred Scott* decision were not an immutable force which could defy the march of history.

As the "War of Northern Aggression" (as it was sometimes called by Southerners) wore on, President Lincoln had several opportunities to appoint Justices to the High Bench who were more in keeping with Northern perspectives, if not with his own political philosophies. John Archibald Campbell, who voted with the majority in *Dred Scott*, resigned from the Court in April 1861 to join the Confederate government. Just a few weeks before, Justice John McLean had died of pneumonia—McLean's contemporary fame resting largely on his vituperative dissent to the *Dred Scott* decision. These events afforded Lincoln two appointment opportunities in addition to an already existing vacancy left by the death of Peter V. Daniel in 1860.

A fourth opportunity occurred midway through the war, in 1863, when the Republican-dominated Congress expanded the Court's bench to a record (and since repealed) ten seats to allow for an appointment from California—the colorful and capable Stephen J. Field. The thought was that some action was needed to secure California's allegiance to the Union, and giving the state a representative on the Supreme Court would help cement the state to the Northern cause. When Chief Justice Taney died in late 1864, Lincoln had a fifth opportunity. On that occasion, he named one of his Republican political rivals, Salmon Portland Chase to the center chair, an act which many have contended was designed to effectively remove Chase from the presidential arena.

The third lecture in "The Supreme Court in the Civil War" series, focused on the Chase Court. Professor G. Edward White, of the University of Virginia, challenged various aspects of the conventional wisdom concerning Chase and his relationship with his fellow Justices.

"The image of Chase as a relative nonentity," according to Professor White, "contrasts sharply with the appraisal of him by contemporaries when he became Chief Justice." White summarizes Chase's tenure as that of " . . . a political strategist within the Court's judicial culture." In explaining this, White compares Chase's ability to influence his colleagues with that of his two immediate predecessors, John Marshall and Roger B. Taney. White's comparison of Taney's attempts to quell dissent in *Dred Scott* with Chase's attempts to preclude a reversal of his "hard currency" advocacy in the *Legal Tender Cases* is particularly illustrative.

In the fourth lecture in the series, Professor Mark E. Neely, Jr., of St. Louis University addressed the war's impact on judicial operations in both the North and the South in a lecture entitled "Justice Embattled."

"War does not provide a congenial environment for coolly reasoned justice," Professor Neely observes, "and the passions of civil war are even less accommodating." Neely's observations are borne out in his detailed discussion of a constitutional confrontation over conscription which nearly split the North in 1863. The episode pitted the Executive and Judicial Branches against one another in a fight over Lincoln's Presidential powers to raise an army by conscription. Though given scant attention in the histories of the Civil War Era, this battle, Neely asserts, held the potential to destroy the North's ability to wage war, and leave a divided country in its wake.

The fact that the Supreme Court remained in operation and continued to hear cases throughout the war, particularly war-related cases, is a testament in itself, to the strength of the Union's constitutional system. Even so, the Court often deferred grave constitutional challenges to the Union war effort until after the war. In the fifth lecture in the series, Professor Harold Hyman, of Rice University examined the Court's docket, offering especially intriguing insights into the little known case of *Lemmon v. New York.*

Lemmon revolved around eight slaves who had been traveling in New York with their owners who were subsequently set free by a state court order enforcing the state's proscription against slavery. For the New York courts to have done otherwise, Professor Hyman concludes, the State would have been acquiescing to the existence of slavery there, and by implication, everywhere. But the slave owners were prepared to argue before the Supreme Court that Article IV offered protection to slaveholders' property rights in "free states." Though the guns of Fort Sumter made the question, and the case moot, had the Taney Court overturned *Lemmon* (not an unreasonable expectation), its so-called "worst self-inflicted wound" [*Dred Scott*] might well have become a little cited footnote to a case which effectively expanded the institution of slavery to every state in the Union.

In the end, of course, the North carried the field in a military sense. But, if the War Between the States was fought over constitutional issues, the real measure of victory is found in which side prevailed in the constitutional arena. The sixth and final part of "The Supreme Court in the Civil War" examined the war's constitutional aftermath in a panel discussion, again conducted by Professor Herman Belz of the University of Maryland, and featured as panelists, Professors Michael Les Benedict of Ohio State University, Randall Kennedy of the Harvard Law School and Earl Maltz of Rutgers School of Law.

This distinguished group considered one of the most heated constitutional debates surrounding the Civil War period—the Supreme Court's enforcement, or lack thereof, depending upon one's perspective, of the Thirteenth, Fourteenth and Fifteenth Amendments. Collectively, these three Amendments were intended to protect the rights of an underprivileged class of newly freed slaves, and to ensure their political enfranchisement. Yet, a century later African-Americans were still being denied voting rights and a multiplicity of other privileges of citizenship, evoking a vigorous and sometimes violent civil rights movement beginning in the mid-twentieth century.

The Supreme Court in the Civil War

The Supreme Court, whose responsibility it was to interpret these new Amendments in the post Civil War era, construed them "more narrowly than their authors had intended," concludes Professor Benedict. Why?

"In the years following their ratification, ambiguities in language and scope of the Civil War Amendments," says Professor Benedict, "led the Supreme Court to interpret the Amendments more narrowly than their authors had intended. The primary reason was that the Amendments had the potential of revolutionizing—in fact eliminating the federal system—a result their authors did not intend."

Fellow panelist Professor Randall Kennedy accepts some of Professor Benedict's conclusions in this regard, but says there is also a strong case to be made that the Court did not work to fulfill the promises of the Reconstruction Amendments.

"For many," says Kennedy, "the history of the Supreme Court's early interpretations of the Reconstruction Amendments is a two-chapter story of tragic betrayal. In chapter one, the Reconstruction Amendments make overdue but nonetheless grand promises that henceforth the federal government would guarantee racial equality. In chapter two, the Supreme Court undermines those promises by construing them too narrowly . . . ."

It is a position that has garnered considerable support among some scholars. But fellow panelist, Earl Maltz, contends this criticism is too sweeping, asserting that, "The Waite Court's reputation as a conservative enemy of federal power to enforce the Reconstruction Amendments has been vastly overstated."

However the Waite Court and its successors responded to the Reconstruction Amendments, it is clear that the Civil War forever changed the constitutional landscape of the United States. It also established constitutional precedents on habeas corpus, freedom of speech and other civil liberties issues, as well as the President's war powers which would carry over into the Twentieth Century and would affect domestic policies in the prosecution of two World Wars. The Society's next special edition of the *Journal of Supreme Court History* will examine this in a volume to be entitled *The Supreme Court in World War Two*.

The Supreme Court and Constitutional Responsibility in the Civil War Era

Herman Belz

This volume on the Supreme Court in the Civil War era is intended, in the most immediate sense, to promote public awareness and understanding of the Court's contribution to American constitutional history, in accordance with the mission of the Supreme Court Historical Society. Because it is the duty and responsibility of the Supreme Court to uphold the Constitution, our purpose, more broadly conceived, is to invite reflection on the Constitution and to promote veneration of it as the nation's fundamental law.

As citizens we are concerned with preserving and maintaining the Constitution. We recognize, moreover, the wisdom of James Madison's teaching on the subject of constitutional maintenance, as expressed in *The Federalist*, no. 49. Discussing the problem of how to maintain a stable government in a political system where the people rule, Madison wrote: "In a nation of philosophers . . . a reverence for the laws would be sufficiently inculcated by the voice of an enlightened reason. But a nation of philosophers is as little to be expected as the philosophical race of kings wished for by Plato. And in every other nation, the most rational government will not find it a superfluous advantage to have the prejudices of the community on its side."

Applying Madison's insight, we state candidly that we wish the prejudices of the community to be on the side of the Constitution. To put the matter in slightly different language, we want public sentiment—the shared convictions and assumptions that in a republican government form the necessary basis for legitimate and authoritative public policy—to rest firm in the conviction that the Constitution is a good in itself, that it has intrinsic as well as instrumental value, and that it embodies principles of reason and justice which at once justify the existence of government and impose limits on government.

How can a simple sheet of parchment, words recorded in a written document, accomplish such a purpose? As we reflect further we are led to inquire what we really mean when we refer to the Constitution. This is a more complicated question than one might suppose, especially if one tried to answer it on the basis of contemporary constitutional theory. Fortunately our historical purpose enables us—indeed it requires us—to think of the Constitution as it was conceived of by its Framers: as a written instrument of government that authorizes the establishment of a limited republican government for the United States of America. Scholar Allan Bloom captures the sense of intellectual simplicity, innovation and virtue that characterized the American idea of constitution when he writes: "It was the pride of the Framers that for the first time in history a nation was founded on written documents that all can read and study and that appeal to the reason of each."[1] If we are to avoid the peril of presentism in our analysis of the constitutional history of the Civil War era, we need to keep this basic understanding in mind.

In the twentieth century constitutional law—as distinguished from the Constitution—has become a dauntingly complex if not arcane field of study. The scope of constitutional law has expanded so that it touches nearly every aspect of national life, from social policy questions of the broadest import to the most local matters involving, for example, the relations of parents and children or the standards of civility that will prevail in a community. In the nineteenth century the scope of constitutional law was not so extensive, nor were constitutional questions so technical in nature as to be confined to the attention of the courts. In order to place our subject in its proper historical context, we need to think of constitutional maintenance, including the settlement of constitutional controversies, as things that were of concern not only to the legislative and executive branches as well as to the judiciary, but also to the average citizen.

To clarify the difference between nineteenth and twentieth century constitutional culture it is helpful to recall the "political questions" doctrine. This doctrine holds that some questions that arise under the Constitution are political in nature and are properly decided by the political branches, while other questions are of a judiciary nature and are properly decided by the courts. An important limitation on judicial power, the doctrine of political questions was central to nineteenth century constitutionalism, but has been all but abandoned in the second half of the twentieth century.

The change that has occurred in the theory of constitutional maintenance and responsibility over the past century can be seen in Professor Bernard Schwartz's treatment of the Civil War as a constitutional crisis, in his recent *History of the Supreme Court*. Professor Schwartz writes: "the Civil War represented an extralegal appeal to force to settle the ultimate legal issue of the nature of the polity. And the issue itself was decided, not by the tribunal to which the resolution of such questions was confided by the Constitution, but by the victorious Union armies."[2] It seems clear that in Professor Schwartz's view the Supreme Court was the tribunal that should have decided the question over which Americans went to war.

On grounds of both political science and history I am inclined to question this understanding of the prevailing canon of constitutional responsibility that existed in the nineteenth century. The question of the nature of the polity—or the nature of the Union, to use more familiar language—was not assigned by the Constitution to the judicial branch and the Supreme Court, but to a different type of "tribunal." If ever there was a momentous "political question" in our constitutional history, this was it. And it was confided, as President Abraham Lincoln argued in his First Inaugural in March 1861, to the "great tribunal, the American people."

A "tribunal" is a seat or court of justice. That Lincoln should refer to "the people" as a tribunal serves to remind us, to quote James Madison again, that "Justice is the end of government" and "the end of civil society." Furthermore, says Madison, justice "ever has been and ever will be pursued until it be obtained, or until liberty be lost in the pursuit." Although Madison was writing in the context of the debate over ratification of the Constitution, his thought applies to recurring problems of government and principles that have significance for other times and places. I suggest that this passage, in which Madison considers the relationship between the pursuit of justice and the existence of liberty, provides a text for thinking about the issues that the "tribunal of the American people" was concerned with in the Civil War era.

In the rapidly expanding United States of the mid-nineteenth century, the requirements of a just social order and the steps to be taken to ensure the preservation of liberty were matters of profound dispute. Slavery existed in fifteen of the thirty-four states; whether it should be extended into the western territories was the immediate question that divided the parties in 1860. The ultimate issue, however, was whether slavery should exist anywhere in the United States, in any of the states where its existence was protected by constitutional guarantees. Was slavery the basis of the republican liberty and the foundation of a just society, as many Southerners insisted, or was slavery the antithesis of liberty and the negation of a just social order, as many Northerners believed?

This was the substantive social issue which, starting in the 1840s with the annexation of Texas, set in motion the events that culminated in the Civil War. Slavery was inextricably linked, however, to two other issues that had long antedated the emergence of slavery as a political issue. These other two issues were no less substantive in their import, and they were constitutional in nature.

The first issue concerned the meaning of "the American people." the tribunal to which Lincoln appealed in his inaugural address. As a description of how the American people were constituted, the words of the preamble—"We the people of the United States"—were shrouded in ambiguity. Were the

At his First Inaugural, President Abraham Lincoln discussed the role of the Supreme Court in American government and politics. He argued that if the decisions of the Supreme Court irrevocably fixed government policy then "the people will have ceased to be their own rulers, having to that extent practically resigned the government into the hands of that eminent tribunal."

people of America an aggregate of individuals constituting political community in the mass, as in a unitary state? Or was the political identity of the people of America that of the people in the several states, the republican communities that constituted the American republic?

The subject of simmering debate since the Nullification crisis of 1833, the problems of defining the legal character of popular sovereignty in the American republic pointed to the second great constitutional issue of the day—the nature of the Union. Was the Union an association of states in the nature of a confederation, from which individual member states could withdraw on their own initiative? Or was the Union a sovereign national government authorized to maintain its own existence by enforcing the laws of the United States against individual citizens, thereby forcing states that would secede to remain in the Union or otherwise assume a rebellious or revolutionary position?

The incommensurability of these constitutional theories was perhaps as clear to contemporaries as it is to the historical observer. The theoretical conundrum could not be detached, however, from sectional, partisan, and ideological passions that rendered the task of constitutional decision making onerous in the extreme. The issues that lay at the core of the controversy were political in nature and rightly belonged to the political branches to decide. And with one major exception, the judicial branch generally respected this limitation.

At no time before the Civil War did the Supreme Court undertake to provide a direct and explicit resolution of the two outstanding constitutional issues of the day. The closest it came was in the *Dred Scott* case when it decided the question of whether slavery could be extended into the territories. The Court said it could, on the ground that "the right of property in a slave is distinctly and expressly affirmed in the Constitution." Therefore, neither Congress nor a territorial legislature possessed constitutional authority to regulate or restrict this right. The Court's decision rested on the compact theory of the Union and the principle of state sovereignty. Only in that limited and indirect sense can it be considered an attempt to settle the question of the nature of the Union.

The *Dred Scott* decision was nevertheless condemned as gratuitous intervention by the Supreme Court into a political question that was none of its business. In recent years the case has been held up as an object lesson for the judiciary on how not to exercise the duty of deciding cases in law and equity arising under the Constitution. In the Court's behalf, however, it should be pointed out that Congress in a series of bills and statutes had for a number of years expressed a desire to let the Justices resolve this contentious policy issue. Then as now, lawmakers were not always eager to exercise their responsibility to decide constitutional questions of a political nature.

Lincoln's reaction to the *Dred Scott* case is instructive on the question of constitutional maintenance and responsibility in the American regime. Lincoln did not question the validity of the Court's holding in the matter of the slave Dred Scott's attempt to secure personal liberty. He held, moreover, that Supreme Court decisions on constitutional questions, "when fully settled, should control not only the particular cases decided, but the general policy of the country." The question of slavery in the territories, however, to say nothing of the larger constitutional issues to which it was related, was not a "fully settled" issue. Lincoln therefore reasoned that the Supreme Court's decision in *Dred Scott* should not be acknowledged and accepted as a political rule of action for the other branches of government. Accordingly the Republican party would try to get the Court to overrule its decision.

In his First Inaugural address Lincoln discussed further the role of the Supreme Court in American government and politics. Acknowledging the view that "constitutional questions are to be decided by the Supreme Court," he disputed this position. "The candid citizens," Lincoln said, "must confess that if the policy of the government, upon vital questions affecting the whole people, is to be irrevocably fixed by decisions of the Supreme Court, the instant they are made, in ordinary litigation between parties in personal actions, the people will have ceased to be their own rulers, having to that extent practically resigned the government into the hands of that eminent tribunal."[3]

On the eve of the Civil War, all could agree that the purpose of the Union was to secure the blessings of liberty to the American people. The northern states identified liberty with the Union and resisted secession as a threat to the Union and the Constitution. The southern states eventually decided that security for liberty and republican government lay outside the Union, in a new confederation of slave-holding states. The papers by Professors Johnson and Kramer that follow explore the ideas of liberty, Union, and popular sovereignty that came into conflict in the 1850s, and proved beyond the ability of any tribunal peacefully to resolve. The fact that these questions continue to command our attention suggests, finally, that however conventional it may be to say, the military outcome of the Civil War did not conclusively and definitively resolve these matters as sources of controversy in constitutional politics, law and theory.

Endnotes

[1] Allan Bloom, ***Confronting the Constitution*** (Washington, D.C.: AEI Press, 1990), p.4.

[2] Bernard Schwartz, ***A History of the Supreme Court*** (New York: Oxford University Press, 1993), p. 126.

[3] Roy P. Basler et al., eds., ***The Collected Works of Abraham Lincoln*** (9 vols., New Brunswick: Rutgers University Press, 1953-55), IV, p. 268.

No Faith in Parchment

Ludwell H. Johnson, III

> I do not stop here, sir, to argue about the constitutionality of this bill; I consider the Constitution a dead letter; I consider it to consist, at this time, of the power of the General Government and the power of the States—that is the Constitution.
> I have no faith in parchment, sir. . . .
> If, with the most approved spring lancets, you draw the last drop of blood from our veins; if, *secundum artem*, you draw the last shilling from our pockets, what are the checks of the Constitution to us? A fig for the Constitution! When the scorpion's sting is probing to the quick, shall we stop to chop logic? . . . There is no magic in this word *union*.[1]

Thus spake John Randolph of Roanoke in 1824—that brilliant, eccentric, eloquent Virginian who had a total irreverence for any man's opinion, and who so often, as here, cut to the heart of the matter. He was opposing a further increase in the tariff, one that would benefit northern manufacturers at the expense of southern agriculturists. To Randolph it was obvious that the contest between North and South was over power, and that government, constitutional or otherwise, would ultimately reflect the realities of power.

The War for Independence had likewise been about power. It had been a struggle over colonial rights and Parliamentary authority. It was a war of secession—of the colonies from the empire, a war by the colonies to become sovereign states. The causes and nature of this contest offer many parallels with the second great war of secession that began eighty-five years later.

Winning independence from Britain merely transferred to this side of the Atlantic the essential constitutional question: what should be the powers of the states, and what should be the powers of any central government that might be established? The first answer, the Articles of Confederation, did little more

John Randolph studied law with his cousin Edmund Randolph, who was then the Attorney General of the United States. He abandoned the study of law to enter the House of Representatives in 1799. Except for the 1814 and 1818 Terms and two years in the Senate from 1825-1827, Randolph served nearly thirty years in the House until 1829.

than institutionalize the functions of the Continental Congress, leaving to each state individually "its sovereignty, freedom, and independence, and every Power, Jurisdiction and right, which is not by this confederation expressly delegated to the United States, in Congress assembled." This first Constitution recognized that the states were the only safe guardians of those rights of natural born Englishmen that the colonists had been contending for, rights that Jefferson's Declaration transmuted into the natural rights of man in the tradition of John Locke, the great philosopher of the Glorious Revolution of 1688.

However, a growing number of citizens came to fear that the Confederation was too weak to protect the infant republic. They formed a lobby sometimes called the Nationalists, an alliance embracing such disparate individuals as James Madison and Alexander Hamilton. Among them were men who, while they had fought for independence, wholeheartedly admired the British social and economic system. The Nationalists succeeded in bringing about the Philadelphia Convention of 1787. As events would prove, the new Constitution drawn up there permitted a significant shift of power from the states to the central government. This was achieved partly by the prohibitions imposed on the states in Article I, Section 10, but more fundamentally by delegating to Congress the power to tax. This power of the purse carried with it political power, the exercise of which would directly or indirectly elicit the opposing constitutional and political theories personified by Jefferson and Hamilton.

Sectional questions, of course, also arose at Philadelphia. They were compromised, beginning what was to be a tradition of accommodation between North and South that would last for two generations. Such compromise was necessary, for as Madison said at the time: "The great danger to our general government *is the great southern and northern interests of the continent, being opposed to each other. Look to the votes in congress, and most of them stand divided by the geography of the country. . . .*" The reasons for this division Madison identified as climate, and especially from the fact of the states "having or not having slaves."[2]

Slavery was then much more an index of economic than of moral differences. The moral question was indeed occasionally raised in the Convention, especially in connection with the slave trade, which was allowed to continue for twenty years at the insistence of South Carolina and Georgia, and also, incidentally, in consideration of those New England businessmen actually engaged in it. This concession was part of a compromise whereby the Convention gave Congress the authority to pass navigation acts for the benefit of northern shipping by a simple majority, an indispensable condition of Northern support for the Constitution.

Other sectional compromises involved slavery not at all or only indirectly. In exchange for prohibiting taxes on exports, something the South feared as giving a northern majority the power of life and death over its agriculture, southern delegates agreed to allow Congress to impose taxes on imports, also by a simple majority, a bargain they would later bitterly regret. And there was the compromise that represented the great unwritten principle of the Constitution, the creation of a balance of power that would prevent either section from oppressing the other. This was the three-fifths ratio provision, which allowed the counting of three-fifths of "other persons" (that is, slaves) in apportioning representation in the House of Representatives and consequently in the electoral college. This would rankle the North for years and would later give plausibility to the notion of a "slave power." Coping with sectional differences, therefore, was necessary to shape a constitution that could win ratification. But in the state ratifying conventions opponents were alarmed more by fear of a stronger central government than by sectional issues. And even they did not fully appreciate the centralizing potentialities of the new system until the Federalists, led by Secretary of the Treasury Hamilton, brought forward their economic program in the 1790s. When their plans were fully revealed, James Madison, that dedicated Nationalist, woke up feeling rather like Baron Frankenstein the morning after. The Hamiltonian dispensation—a funded national debt, assumption of state debts, a central bank, navigation acts, tariffs—used the power of the purse to draw influence and political strength to the center in an attempt to recreate on these shores an American version of the British mercantile system and social polity.

Madison and Jefferson and their allies came to see Hamilton and his faction as Anglophiles and covert monarchists, therefore as a menace to the liberties the Revolution had been fought to secure. They reverted to the tactics of the 1770s, which had striven to guard historic rights by denying the authority of King and Parliament in certain important respects. They took as their guiding political principle limiting the power of the federal government and thus enhancing that of the states—strict construction of the Constitution, with nullification or secession held in reserve as a last resort.

Because the Hamiltonian program was highly sectional in its effects, favoring the North at the expense of the South, this battle to defend liberty was not only a struggle of the states against the federal government, but of South against North. The defense of liberty, the rights of the states, and the safety and welfare of the South came to be indistinguishable, and that defense was couched in ideological, economic, and political, as well as in constitutional terms. More and more, the contest between Republicans and Federalists and their respective successors came to be seen in terms of that unwritten article of the Constitution, the maintenance of an acceptable sectional balance of political power. This idea of a balance was widely recognized. For instance, at the Hartford Convention of 1814, New Englanders complained that the original balance had been upset and should be restored, and they proposed amendments to the Constitution that would have eliminated the three-fifths ratio and in other ways put limits on their opponents, who were, they believed, dominating the nation under the seemingly endless succession of Virginian Presidents.

During the early years of the nineteenth century, a sectional equilibrium in the Senate was maintained as new states came into the Union. As Madison had observed, a state's latitude and the presence or absence of slavery were seen as factors strongly influencing the position a state would take on economic and political questions. The Missouri controversy of 1819-1821 clearly pivoted on this issue. Jefferson expressed contempt for the old Federalists who tried to make the exclusion of slavery from Missouri a

Representatives of the New England states met at the Hartford Convention to consider measures that would strengthen Federalism during an era of Republican domination of both domestic and foreign affairs. The work of the Convention ended abruptly with the signing of the Treaty of Ghent, which concluded the War of 1812.

moral question. It was, he said, a "mere party trick." The Federalists were "taking advantage of the virtuous feelings of the people to effect a division of parties by a geographical line," having failed to obtain power "by rallying partisans to the principles of monarchism." There was, said Jefferson, no moral issue, for allowing slavery in Missouri would not make slaves of any who were not already slaves, and would in fact facilitate emancipation by spreading the black population more thinly.

The use of the moral issue of slavery as a means to achieve political success and economic advantage was becoming more explicit. As an example, had Alabama not been admitted in 1819, a new, higher tariff bill would have passed in 1820. At a July 4 celebration that year in Harrisburg, Pennsylvania, a stronghold of protectionism, a toast was proposed to "National Industry—It is held in fetters by the iron grasp of slavery; may it soon burst the bands, and give food, health and happiness to a virtuous people."[3] In other words, unless slavery was contained, a higher tariff was doomed.

With each new acquisition of territory and with the proposed admission of each new state, the focus on slavery became more intense and the relationship between northern prosperity and limiting slavery, which meant limiting southern political power, seemed self-evident. In 1846, following the defeat of several legislative measures dear to the hearts of northern interests, Representative David Wilmot of Pennsylvania proposed that slavery be barred from any territory that might be gained from the war with Mexico. A Chicago newspaper showed plainly what lay behind the growing opposition to the extension of slavery. In an editorial on the defeat of a rivers and harbors bill by Southern votes, it charged:

> The lives and property of the freemen of the North, her free laborers, sailors, and those passing to and fro upon her great Lakes and Rivers are of no concern to the Government. . . . The North can and will be no longer hoodwinked. If no measures for protection and improvement of anything North or West are to be suffered by our Southern masters, if we are to be downtrodden, and all our cherished interests crushed by them, . . . [then] the North and West will . . . see . . . that the power to oppress shall not again be entrusted to men who have shown themselves to be slaveholders, but not Americans. . . . The fiat has gone forth—Southern rule is at an end.[4]

By this time, slavery had come to stand for every issue between the sections, and, thanks to the great religious revivals of the 1820s and 1830s, it was now presented more and more as a strictly moral question. This would at last make compromise on the underlying differences between North and South impossible, because moral questions offer only a choice between right and wrong. In this way the South, in order to preserve what it regarded as the minimum share of political power needed to protect itself, came to pin everything on the constitutional right of slave owners to take their slaves into the territories. Not that they expected them to go there—rather it was a test of the North's willingness to forbear to use the power of the majority to deny to the South the equality of rights it no longer had the votes to vindicate.

History can sometimes be unkind. The weapons of states' rights and state sovereignty that Jefferson used to defend the political and civil liberties secured by the Revolution now came to be the weapons of those who no longer saw slavery as, at best, a necessary evil, as Jefferson had done, but who, like Calhoun, upheld it as a positive good. Yet the latter also saw themselves as championing those same liberties Jefferson had defended. They found themselves in the awkward position of defending liberty by defending slavery. And when the war came, they could say, as a Confederate poem had it, "Yes, call us rebels, 'tis the name our patriot fathers bore."

In the decade of the 1850s, a growing number of Southerners came to believe that the Constitution was no longer a sufficient shield, given their dwindling strength in Congress. Their fears were heightened in 1859 by John Brown's attempt to incite a race war. Then in 1860 Abraham Lincoln won election as the candidate of a wholly northern, anti-southern party with the announced intention of forever curbing southern political power and reforming the Constitution to bring it in line with Republican consolidationist doctrines. On December 20 the people of South Carolina decided the time had

John C. Calhoun of South Carolina served his state and his country throughout his career, in Congress, as Vice-President, as Secretary of War and as Secretary of State. He also served as the political leader of the South, arguing that the South must be protected from the tyranny of the Northern majority.

come to seek safety in independence, and for guidance they turned to those patriot forefathers. As their state convention explained:

> The Revolution of 1776 turned upon one great principle, self-government—and self-taxation, the criterion of self-government. Where the interests of two people united together under one Government, are different, each must have the power to protect its interests . . . or they cannot be free. . . . Great Britain was desirous of carrying out the policy of all nations towards their Colonies, of making them tributary to her wealth and power . . . . The North American Colonies saw their interests, political and commercial, sacrificed by such a policy. . . . To make them a part of a consolidated Empire, the Parliament of Great Britain determined to assume the power of legislating for the Colonies in all cases whatsoever. Our ancestors resisted the pretension. They refused to be a part of the consolidated Government of Great Britain. The Southern States now stand exactly in the same position towards the Northern States that the colonies did towards Great Britain.[5]

And so to escape oppression at the hands of superior power, South Carolina exercised her sovereignty and withdrew from the Union.

Before following her out, the other southern states made one last effort to obtain ironclad constitutional guarantees by way of amendments. When the Republican leadership, headed by President-elect Lincoln, blocked all compromise, six more Deep South states seceded and formed the Confederate States of America. Then Lincoln's decision to use force to put down secession drove out four states of the Upper South, which then joined the new nation.

The right to secede rested on the doctrine of state sovereignty. Sovereignty can be defined as supreme political power. The doctrine was quite simple. The states were sovereign political communities. They had delegated certain powers to the Federal government, thus creating the union called the United States, but in so doing they did not surrender sovereignty. Since sovereignty is by definition supreme, they, or any one of them, could take back those delegated powers, thereby leaving the union and resuming their original independent status.

In outline, the southern argument in support of the doctrine is likewise simple. It goes as follows: The only organic connection between the colonies during the Colonial period was allegiance to the sovereign power, Britain. The Treaty of Paris of 1783 recognized each of the colonies to be "free, sovereign and independent States." Their freedom and sovereignty were also acknowledged by the Articles of Confederation. As for the Constitution, it did the same by providing that it would take effect when ratified by nine of the thirteen states then forming the United States. Further proof of state sovereignty was the fact that after eleven states had ratified and the Constitution had gone into effect, North Carolina remained out of the Union for months and Rhode Island for two years as independent republics.

The only remaining question to be answered was

whether a state surrendered its sovereignty by the act of ratification. Southerners marshaled voluminous evidence to show that nothing in the Constitution or the ratifying process effected such a fundamental change. Nowhere was it suggested that the separate sovereignties of the people of the respective states had been merged into one sovereignty embracing the people of all the states without distinction, a change too momentous to be established by mere inference. Those interested in the details of the argument may refer to the works of John C. Calhoun and Alexander H. Stephens, among others.

It must be said that the Southerners had much the better case, at least in my humble opinion. Not until the post-bellum years did the Supreme Court face the issue squarely, when in *Texas v. White* (1869) Chief Justice Salmon P. Chase declared that the Constitution looked to "an indestructible Union, composed of indestructible States." His brief argument was no better than the ones Southerners had demolished long ago, and as for "indestructible" states, the Court had only to turn its collective gaze across the Potomac to see Military District Number One where the "indestructible" state of Virginia had once been. That district starkly illustrated the truth of what John Randolph had said forty-five years before: "I consider the Constitution a dead letter; I consider it to consist . . . of the power of the General Government and the power of the States—that is the Constitution." The power of the general government, put forth in four years of bloody war and more years of military rule, had rewritten the Constitution. "I have no faith in parchment, sir," Randolph had said. How right he was.

Endnotes

[1] Frederick Jackson Turner, ***Rise of the New West, 1819-1829*** (New York: Collier Books, 1962), 171.

[2] Max Farrand, ed., ***The Records of the Federal Convention of 1787*** (New Haven and London: Yale University Press, 1966), I, 476, 486.

[3] Glover Moore, ***The Missouri Controversy, 1819-1821*** (Lexington, Ky.: University of Kentucky Press, 1953), 329.

[4] Avery Craven, ***Edmund Ruffin, Southerner: A Study in Secession*** (New York: D. Appleton and Co., 1932), 264-65, n. 6.

[5] John Amasa May and John Reynolds Faunt, ***South Carolina Secedes*** (Columbia: University of South Carolina Press, 1960), 83.

Federalism in Antebellum America: The View From the North

Larry Kramer[1]

The central issue that defined legal and political debate from the time the Constitution was ratified until the end of the Civil War was federalism, or the relationship between state and federal governments. Federalism was not always the explicit subject of debate, of course. Issues like slavery, banks, tariffs, and internal improvements were what people fought about. But the relationship between the state and federal governments defined views on these issues, as well as just about everything else that happened during this period. The question was, who has final say: the states, speaking through their legislatures, or the federal government, speaking through Congress and, eventually, the Supreme Court? And that question, in turn, boiled down to a question of primacy: which came first, the nation or the states? Were we one nation divided for some purposes into states, or many small nations united for some purposes into one?

Daniel Webster, in addition to his distinguished career as a Senator, was considered among the nation's most talented legal advocates—despite winning fewer than half of his cases before the Supreme Court.

The Northern position, which is to say the position held by a majority of Northerners in the antebellum years, was the nationalist position. One finds it presented in many contexts in the early years of the republic, though not always or only by Northerners. It is implicit, for example, in Virginian John Marshall's opinions for the Supreme Court in *Gibbons v. Odgen*[2] and *McCulloch v. Maryland*,[3] as well as the response to the Virginia and Kentucky Resolutions.[4] But the best early presentation of the nationalist position, the one that set the stage for later debate, is Daniel Webster's reply to Robert Hayne in the Senate.

For those of you who aren't familiar with it, the Webster-Hayne debate took place in 1830.[5] It began with the question of how to dispose of public lands in the West. Revenue from the sale of these lands was pledged to retiring the public debt, which was almost gone by 1830, soon to be replaced by a surplus. Various proposals had been made to change land policy as a result of this development, including one to cede the lands to the states. Not everyone, however, was anxious simply to get rid of these holdings. Calling attention to the fact that seventy-two million acres of land already surveyed remained unsold, Samuel Foot of Connecticut introduced a resolution to study whether it made sense to suspend the surveys, abolish the Surveyor General's office, and close some land offices. This provoked a response from Thomas Hart Benton of Missouri, a former enemy but now close ally of Andrew Jackson. Benton had proposed legislation to complete the survey work and sell Western land at drastically reduced prices. Attacking Foot for wanting to "pauperize" the West, Benton accused "the East" of conspiring to frustrate westward expansion with a tightfisted land policy. He asked for support from Southern senators.

This was a calculated political move on Benton's part, seeking to shift sectional alliances in the Senate to reflect the popular alignment that elected President Jackson. And Robert Hayne of South Carolina stood and supported Benton, linking federal policy on public lands with tariffs and the American System as examples of Eastern exploitation. Near the end of Hayne's oration, Webster apparently wandered into the Senate chamber. Webster may have been angered to hear Hayne make this speech, having just the day before done Hayne a favor by introducing a bill for federal aide to a South Carolina railroad. In any event, Webster rose to reply, and the debate took off from there—turning in the next several days to tariffs, internal improvements, slavery and, ultimately, the nature of the Union itself.

Even at the time, it was generally conceded that Webster's eloquent defense of the Union had crushed Hayne. Webster didn't persuade anyone, of course. Southerners didn't hear Webster and realize, "by golly, that the nationalists are right after all". But Webster did make the case for the importance and supremacy of the Union, establishing its foundations for future debate and future reference. And no one but Abraham Lincoln ever did it better.

Webster's position, in a nutshell, was that states were subordinate to the federal government in the sense that they had no power to override its actions. The Constitution is the fundamental law of one people, not a compact of states. In Webster's words, it is "the people's constitution, the people's Government; made for the people; made by the people and answerable to the people."[6] And in that last clause, "answerable to the people," was an implicit but unmistakable "only"—answerable *only* to the people, meaning the people of the whole United States.

Webster rested this claim on three arguments. First, he made a legal argument: that the text of the Constitution itself established the primacy of the federal government over the states. Later politicians would rely on the first clause of the Constitution, "We the People," to make this claim—a questionable argument because, as Professor Herman Belz points out, the identity of this "People" is not entirely clear. Earlier drafts of the Constitution said "We the People of . . ." and listed the states. This list was removed at the Convention by the Committee on Detail, but we do not know whether this was done to make clear that it was the people of the nation who were acting or because the long list of states was deemed clumsy and unnecessary; there were men of both views in Philadelphia and at the various ratifying conventions.

So Webster didn't rely on the preamble but instead made a more lawyerly argument. He pointed to the Supremacy Clause, which says that federal law is supreme and that state officials are bound by it, and he combined this with the clause in Article III giving the Supreme Court jurisdiction over constitutional issues. According to Webster, these two clauses together make clear that when there are questions in dispute—particularly questions regarding the scope of federal power—final say is vested in an agency of the federal government.[7] (Of course, Webster just assumed that if the Supreme Court has authority to decide, that authority must be final—a point that was established with respect to the particular case but that remained contested with respect to the implications of a judicial interpretation for other cases.)

Webster's second argument, and one to which he devoted more time in the debate, was pragmatic. The Southern view of the Union as nothing more than a compact among independent states, Webster contended, was too narrow and confining for the ambitious people of the United States. As states' rights advocates would have it, the Federal Government could not act unless everyone benefited

James Madison wrote persuasively that federalism would help to secure liberty in the *Federalist Papers*. More than forty years later Daniel Webster argued that diffuse reciprocity among the regions of the nation would do the same.

and the benefits were distributed in a roughly equal manner; Congress could not authorize a canal from New York to Ohio and finance it with federal dollars because this would do nothing for South Carolina. But that is true only if one insists on seeing New York, Ohio, and South Carolina as independent societies with independent interests. If they view themselves as part of one nation, then what benefits one part may be seen as benefiting the whole.[8]

Webster did not explain this argument as well as he might have, but read in context, Webster is advocating what international relations theorists today usefully call "diffuse reciprocity."[9] Rather than measure each action of the national government to see if it specifically provides benefits to everyone (specific reciprocity), Webster urges us to look at the cumulative effects of many actions over time. We are all part of one people, he says, and we should trust that in the long run all will gain and all will be better off. Today, one section benefits; tomorrow another; later, another still. And the benefits to each section in its turn are greater if other sections have already been made stronger: stronger industry in the North means bigger markets for Southern cotton which, in turn, increases demand for Western agriculture, and so on. The interdependent nature of the American economy means that freedom to help different sections at different times will produce greater prosperity for the nation as a whole.

Webster adds that diffuse reciprocity among the various sections of the nation will also help secure liberty. James Madison made the most well-known argument about federalism and liberty, contending in the *Federalist* Nos. 10 and 51 that self-interested factions would never be able to capture and control the national government in an extended republic. This was not Webster's argument. He did not repudiate Madison's claim; he just didn't rely on it. Rather, Webster reasoned that there will be less strife if we recognize our shared interests and trust in our ability to improve our lives by giving aid to different parts at different times. Moreover, as a good New England capitalist, Webster saw the connection between liberty and prosperity—that the best protection of liberty is economic health and that the confining Southern view would retard economic growth. Real prosperity depended on the ability to take joint national action, as reflected in measures like tariffs, internal improvements, and the national bank. And with prosperity would come liberty.

Webster's third argument was a romantic one. The Union, said Webster, is a great experiment: an experiment in liberty, an experiment in self-government, an experiment in the ability of a people to act virtuously and forgo petty jealousies. But let Webster speak for himself here. It is important to have a sense of this remarkable speaker and also to appreciate the nature of debate in the nineteenth century Senate. Webster reportedly gave these speeches from two or three pages of brief notes he had scratched out the night before. Most of his reply to Hayne is actually extemporaneous. So listen to Webster exhort his colleagues and the public to appreciate the Union:

> While the Union lasts, we have high, exciting, gratifying prospects spread out before us, for us and our children. Beyond that, I seek not to penetrate the veil. God grant that, in my day, at least, that curtain may not rise. God grant that, on my vision, never may be opened what lies behind. When my eyes shall be turned to behold, for the last time, the sun in heaven, may I not see him shining on the broken and dishonored fragments of a once glorious Union; on States dissevered, discordant, belligerent; on a land rent with civil feuds, or drenched, it may be, in fraternal blood! Let their last feeble and lingering glance, rather, behold the gorgeous ensign of the republic, now known and honored throughout the earth, still full high advanced, its arms and trophies streaming in their original lustre, not a stripe erased or polluted, nor a single star obscured, bearing for its motto no such miserable interrogatory as, What is all this worth? Nor those other words of delusion and folly, Liberty first, and Union afterwards; but every where, spread all over in characters of living light, blazing on all its ample folds, as they float over the sea and over the land, and in every wind under the whole heavens, that other sentiment, dear to every true American heart,—Liberty *and* Union, now and forever, one and inseparable.[10]

No one ever did it better, except maybe Lincoln, at Gettysburg.

* * *

Webster's reply to Hayne contains most of the substance of the Northern position. Certainly no one added much to the argument in later years, apart from an historical claim. And, once again, Lincoln did this best, both in his debates with Stephen Douglas while running for the Senate in 1858 and in his first inau-

President Abraham Lincoln argued in his debates with Stephen Douglas in 1858 and 1860 that the states never existed separately but had been an imperfect Union in 1774 that was formalized in 1776 with the Declaration of Independence.

gural. According to Lincoln, the states never existed independently. The colonies formed an imperfect union, but a union nevertheless, in 1774, when they convened the first Continental Congress. This was made official with the Declaration of Independence in 1776, which created the Union and the states simultaneously. But, Lincoln held, it was always one national people acting. The states never existed as fully independent sovereigns, a point shown by the fact that they never exercised all the powers a sovereign was normally held to possess. For example, and most obviously, the states never had legitimate foreign relations power. Dealing with other nations (at least legitimate dealing) was always done jointly through a national assembly.

I want to clarify a few points about the understanding of sovereignty at the time of the founding and later. The Constitution was based on the idea that sovereignty resided in the people, i.e., popular sovereignty. The people could allocate this authority as they chose: they could give it all to a national government, they could give it all to their states, or they could divide it between the two, which is what they did. This understanding was critical in the debates over ratifying the Constitution. In the early stages of the Convention, James Madison and Alexander Hamilton (together with some other proponents of centralized authority) tried to abolish the independent sovereignty of the states. They recognized rather quickly that this was not politically feasible, which left them with a problem: the best political science of the day held that you could have only one supreme legislative power in any nation. How, then, to preserve independent states while creating an independent national government able to legislate directly? Popular sovereignty was the answer. There was not more than one sovereign over the people in a federal system, because the people themselves were sovereign. And the people could divide their sovereignty as they chose. But, the argument went, it was one people of the whole United States dividing sovereignty between a national government, which would govern all of them, and state governments, whose authority was restricted to smaller communities within.

* * *

This argument about the nature of the Union and the primacy of the federal government within its proper sphere (which included the power to define the scope of federal power) conditioned the Northern response to every major controversy up to and including the Civil War. Northern politicians and the Northern public were not fighting about federalism, of course. They were fighting about tariffs and regulating the economy and slavery. But their fights were shaped by their understanding of this basic problem of the nature of the Union.

Let me run quickly through some of the major controversies to illustrate the nationalist argument in context. The South maintained that tariffs were unconstitutional because they operated as a tax on one region for the benefit of another. In Southern eyes, tariffs were enacted to benefit manufacturing interests in the North, especially the Northeast; Southern agriculture and Southern consumers were hurt, because raising the price of British textiles reduced demand, which reduced production, which reduced British demand for Southern cotton. Northern politicians replied that strengthening U.S. industry would eventually benefit everyone. It might shift demand for Southern cotton from England to the North, but making American commerce stronger would make everyone more prosperous in the long run. And, of course, there was nothing to prevent Southerners from opening their own factories.

The dispute over tariffs led directly to the controversy over nullification. Given the Northern position, it was obviously nonsensical to talk about state "interposition" and nullification. States could not be final judges of supreme federal law (except by amendment) because they had no power over the federal government. Only the federal government's own agencies, here the Supreme Court, could decide whether a federal statute was constitutional. Nor, from the Northern perspective, did the Virginia and Kentucky Resolutions say anything different: the Resolutions suggested that states might organize opposition to the Federal Government, might try to force reconsideration in Congress or the Supreme Court. But states could not affirmatively block or interfere with the enforcement of federal law. (This may even have been a correct interpretation of the Resolutions, though Jefferson and Madison were deliberately obscure at the time.[11])

The argument with respect to internal improvements is basically the same as the argument for tariffs. Internal improvements were justified as measures designed to strengthen the national economy by making it easier for commerce to move from state to state, eventually redounding to benefit the whole people of the United States. The Bank of the United States was justified on similar grounds.

As one moves on in time, the debate turns more and more to slavery, particularly the power of Congress to regulate slavery in the territories. This was crucial to the South, because as new states were added the South faced the prospect of losing its voice in national politics. It was also a relatively straightforward matter from the Northern perspective. The territories were held by the United States. They were not, as Southerners argued, lands held in trust for the benefit of the states. They belonged to the whole people of the United States, and were therefore subject to regulation by the voice that spoke for the whole nation, which was Congress. Decisions about how to use the territories could therefore be made by the people of the United States in Congress assembled, without limits imposed to protect some fictional notion of states' rights.

It is not really difficult to work out the arguments on any particular issue, and on all of them the Northern position was relatively consistent. Secession, of course, was the culmination of this string of controversies. But here, too, the Northern argument was straightforward: states could not dissolve the Union because states did not make the Union. Only the people, acting as a constituent whole, could dissolve the Union. There was, to be sure, a traditional right of revolution (Lincoln called it a moral right in his First Inaugural): a people so badly treated by its government that its natural rights were abridged could rebel. But the conditions for exercising that right most definitely were not met in the case of the South; not even Southerners took that position. Hence, secession was unlawful.

* * *

Were the Northerners right? As Professor Herman Belz observes, the Union armies answered that question for all practical purposes. So instead of examining the merits, I want to ask whether this legal controversy mattered. The people of the period treated the question of whether the states or the nation came first as a question of fact, and they treated it as a question of fact that mattered a lot—as if the legal argument could provide answers to their problems. I think they were wrong, but in examining why we learn some important lessons about the role of law in political debate.

The problem is that the debate was based on erroneous assumptions. The question of primacy was *not* a question of fact, at least not one that could ever be answered; and even if an answer could have been found, it would not have provided guidance on the problems facing the United States in the antebellum years. As for the first point, the difficulty is not that historical questions can never be resolved. But this particular question cannot be resolved on the available record, and to pretend otherwise is a fiction. The document presented to the public in 1787 deliberately fudged the question, which was too divisive and did not need to be resolved in order to get done what needed to be done. If you read the *Federalist*, for example, you see that Publius is all over the map on this issue. Indeed, arguments going every which way are found on both sides throughout the ratification debates. Clearly the participants had strong views, but there was nothing close to consensus on the matter, which remained unsettled. So nobody "won" this debate and there is nothing to find—only an ongoing controversy about which view better fits the evolving Union.[12]

This brings me to my second observation—that nothing follows from the argument anyway. I've always been surprised that no one pointed out how, starting from either the position of the South or that of the North, one could easily reach any conclusion urged from the other: Even if the states did come first, that doesn't tell us how much sovereignty they surrendered, and the record contains more than enough evidence to find that the states surrendered all that was necessary to support the Northern position. Or even if the nation came first, the people might have limited the national government to preserve state sovereignty along the lines suggested by Southern politicians. And, again, there is more than enough in the record to support this conclusion. One might have expected somebody to stand up and say, "Of course we need to decide what to do about slavery, about tariffs, about internal improvements. But we're not going to find a solution by asking whether the nation or the states came first, because nothing follows from the answer to that question."

That resolution of this question could not answer the problems of antebellum American (or those of America today) should not come as a surprise. Law seldom dictates the final outcome of powerfully divisive political disputes. Had either side prevailed in the debate—obtaining favorable decisions in the Supreme Court, for example—the Civil War would still have come, and the North would still have won.[13] As Professor Ludwell Johnson suggests, the forces that produced the Civil War, that led to secession, that inspired the controversies and compromises of the period were much too powerful to be allayed by legal argument. In situations like this, the passion of politics must be expected to twist and distort the logic of legal analysis.

Law nonetheless matters. It matters because, as the people and politicians of the nineteenth century understood, it is essential in a constitutional democracy to have a plausible legal justification for one's position. That's why we see this debate. Law bends politics too. Even if the bottom line would have come out the same, the route taken to get there *was* affected by this legal argument. And for the people involved, the route that produces a result is as important as the result itself, because the journey as much as the end is what constitutes their lives.

Endnotes

[1] Professor of Law, New York University. The text of this article is based on a transcription of oral comments.

[2] 22 U.S. (9 Wheat.) 1 (1824).

[3] 17 U.S. (4 Wheat.) 316 (1819).

[4] *See* Stanley Elkins & Eric McKitrick, ***The Age of Federalism*** 691-754 (1993); Noble E. Cunningham, ***The Jeffersonian Republicans: The Formation of Party Organization*** (1950); Adrienne Koch, ***Jefferson and Madison: The Great Collaboration*** (1964).

[5] For a more detailed but very readable discussion of the debate and its background, *see* Merrill D. Peterson, ***The Great Triumvirate*** 170-83 (1987).

[6] ***21st Cong., 1st Sess. Register of Debates*** 74 (1830) [hereafter ***Register of Debates***].

[7] ***Register of Debates*** at 78-79.

[8] ***Register of Debates*** at 62-68. Webster must have enjoyed this argument, which undoubtedly made Hayne squirm given Hayne's request—through Webster—for federal aid to a South Carolina railroad.

[9] *See, e.g.,* Robert O. Keohane, ***International Institutions and State Power*** 134 (1989).

[10] ***Register of Debates*** at 80.

[11] *See* authorities cited *supra* note 3.

[12] This being so, it is remarkable how many people today still want to resolve the primacy question as a question of historical fact. *See, e.g., U.S. Term Limits v. Thornton*, 115 S.CT. 1842 (1995), especially the dissent by Justice Clarence Thomas; Samuel H. Beer, T***o Make a Nation: The Rediscovery of American Federalism*** (1993).

[13] Hence, the claim that *Dred Scott* helped bring on the Civil War has always seemed silly to me. Had the Court reached the opposite conclusion, upholding Congress's power to regulate slavery in the territories, nothing would have changed except those who praised the decision and those who condemned it would have switched positions.

Taney, Lincoln And The Constitutional Conversation*

Phillip Paludan

No other period in the nation's history tested the Constitution so profoundly, none other interrelated so well the conversation implicit in the Constitutional system between means and ends, between ideals and process, between equal justice and the rule of law, as the Civil War era. My focus will be predominantly on the *Dred Scott* case, when the stakes of the Civil War in constitutional terms were defined.

I will focus on the ways in which Roger B. Taney and Abraham Lincoln responded to the greatest threat to the Constitution and self-government in the Civil War years—the fact of slavery.

To do this my inquiry will take several steps. First this paper will ask what is the nature of slavery's threat to the constitutional system? Then it will look at how Taney responded to the threat and will place his response within his view of the original intent of the Framers of the Constitution. Then it will offer another view of what the Framers intended—not so much an alternate view but rather an additional view of original intent. Finally, I'll bring Lincoln into the story and show how he responded to the threat of slavery and how he saw the original intent of the Framers and what he did to make the constitutional system an ongoing conversation.

The first papers in this volume focused on disunion and on the northern and southern arguments about the right to secede, to divide the union. The focus of my paper is the reason that argument took place at all, slavery. Slavery was at the core of every state sovereignty statement certainly from the 1830s on and probably before. Only slave states seceded. Here is the testimony of the Vice President of the Confederacy, Alexander Stephens, on the difference between the creation of the United States in the 1780s and the creation of the Confederacy in 1861: "The prevailing ideas entertained by [Jefferson] and most of the leading statesmen at the time of the formation [of the] old Constitution, were that the enslavement of the African was in violation of the laws of nature; that it was wrong in principle, socially, morally, and politically. . . . Our new government is founded upon exactly the opposite idea; its foundations are laid, its cornerstone rests upon the great truth that, the Negro is not equal to the white man; that slavery-subordination to the superior race—is his natural and normal condition." Slavery can't be kept out of the discussion of Civil War.

And it certainly can't be kept out of a discussion of the Constitution in the Civil War era. For slavery was there in Philadelphia when the Constitution was written. It was, as one scholar has called it, "The Witch at the Christening."[1] And it was always slavery which threatened to kill the child, the Constitution, created at Philadelphia.

Slavery posed a more obvious threat to the Union. If southern states could not be assured that their "peculiar institution" would be secure and would be able to expand, they were ready to secede, to create the "Disunited States of America." But more was threatened than dividing the nation. If secession succeeded, the peaceful process established by the Constitution for changing governments would have failed. The precedent would have been established: losers of elections don't have to win the next election for their views to prevail; they can abandon the system and set up their own; and they can do this by gunfire. If

Senator Charles Sumner of Massachusetts was brutally caned in the Senate chamber in 1856 by Representative Preston Brooks of South Carolina. The beating came two days after Senator Sumner delivered a two-day oration berating the South for its "crime against Kansas," and singling out Senator Andrew Butler of South Carolina. Senator Butler, who was the uncle of Representative Brooks, was not present to respond to the accusations of Senator Sumner.

they did this successfully then the constitutional process of the founding years would have failed.

Secession backed by armed force was the ultimate cataclysm for the United States. But connected with it and indeed precipitating it was another fact, less well appreciated. The nation was heading for that cataclysm because of the power of slavery to shut down another part of the constitutional process, the built-in process of settling differences through discussion and negotiation. Slavery was the greatest threat by far to the nation and the constitution. But rather than facing that threat and discussing how the threat might be reduced or eliminated, slavery's defenders were shutting down debate. Defenders of slavery were so frightened at the prospect of losing slavery that throughout the prewar decades proponents of slavery had mobbed and killed abolitionist speakers and writers, and ostracized southern opponents of slavery. They had stifled debate in Congress by passing gag rules in 1836 and 1840 that tabled all antislavery petitions. And most notoriously, slavery had challenged antislavery on May 22, 1856, when Preston Brooks of South Carolina nearly beat Senator Sumner to death for making an antislavery speech on the floor of Congress.

But slavery posed a further threat to the political-constitutional system. And that threat was more dangerous because it was more subtle. The threat was this: in the 1850s especially, two of the nation's most cherished ideas and institutions were being captured by slavery. Democracy and the Constitution were being turned into pro-slavery ideals.

Nineteenth-century Americans defined themselves by democracy and the Constitution. They were a self governing people in practically every aspect of their daily life. They voted in numbers as high as eighty percent and ninety percent in elections, they created governments daily as they expanded across the continent, they held elections almost every month somewhere in the nation, they rotated offices constantly.

Their political debates were nothing if not debates over the Constitution. Self government was America; it was "cosa nostra," "our thing."

But in the prewar era an effort was underway, sometimes conscious, at times unconscious, to capture those ideals for slavery. First, consider how democracy was under siege. In 1854 Senator Stephen Douglas of Illinois wanted to open the west for railroad development. He needed southern votes. To get them he was ready to allow slavery to expand into the west. Congress had outlawed slavery there in 1820, but with the Kansas-Nebraska Act, Congress repealed the Missouri Compromise. The act threatened to expand slavery across hundreds of thousands of miles of territory. But perhaps more threatening was Douglas' justification for it.

Douglas argued for expansion by insisting that "popular sovereignty" gave the people of any state or territory the right to enslave black people. Democracy, Stephen Douglas style, allowed and even nurtured racism. Certainly in his debates with Lincoln, Douglas played the race card constantly and appealed to the worst angels of his white audience. Speaking words endorsed by his party, Douglas assured white Americans that democracy was perfectly compatible with slavery. Devotees of democracy, and there were millions of them, could rest easy on the slavery question. They didn't have to discuss it any more. Democracy could mean slavery.

Meanwhile the Constitution was being turned into a pro-slavery document. Chief Justice Roger B. Taney agreed with Douglas that democracy and slavery were quite compatible. But Taney went farther. In a series of opinions culminating in *Dred Scott v. Sandford* in 1857, the Chief Justice insisted that slavery was a permanent feature of the Constitution, one that could not be changed because the Constitution had to be interpreted in terms of what was intended in 1787 when the Framers wrote the document. According to Taney, that world was relentlessly racist, and its racism was housed in the Constitution forever.

These two positions, that democratic government and the Constitution both endorsed slavery, significantly threatened the rule of law in the nation. For they denied that there was a legal means to end slavery. Taney's *Dred Scott* opinion was a direct blow against burgeoning antislavery sentiment in the country. That sentiment had created a new political party in 1854 and within two years, that party, the Republican party had achieved a popular majority of *northern* votes in the 1856 presidential election. But Taney said that the electoral process could not choose against slavery. The main plank of the Republican party,—"no expansion of slavery"—violated the Constitution. And Senator Douglas agreed with that. Endorsing the *Dred Scott* opinion and the Supreme Court's authority, Douglas declared for judicial supremacy, "It is the fundamental principle of the judiciary," Douglas said, "that its decisions are final.[2]

Now note the dangerous consequence of combining Douglas' and Taney's positions. Slavery is clearly the greatest danger to the survival of the United States. But democratic self government can not and should not challenge slavery, because the Constitution protects and defends slavery. What did that leave as a means of confronting the threat? Essentially it left radical abolitionists as slavery's challengers. And these were men and women who burned the Constitution and called it a "covenant with death and an agreement with hell." They presented the only alternative to the power of slavery. Civil disobedience and not the order of law was the only way to uproot the nation's most evil and dangerous institution.

That was the meaning if Taney was right about the Constitution. If Taney was right, law-respecting Americans would have to make a choice that the philosopher-statesman Goethe had described as the French Revolution overtook Europe: "If I had to choose between disorder and injustice, I would choose injustice."[3] And with the utmost irony, if Taney was right then Thurgood Marshall's statement made during the bicentennial of the Constitution, would also be right. Marshall who had spent his professional life issuing constitutional challenges to racism, doubted in 1987 that blacks should celebrate that bicentennial. Americans were "commemorating the wrong document," Marshall said. The constitution of 1787 was a "defective" document that intentionally enslaved blacks and denied rights to women.[4]

Was Taney right? Well, he was both right and wrong. Reading the Constitution the way Taney read it, he was right. But there are other ways to read the document and Abraham Lincoln was going to illustrate how that might be done.

The Constitutional Conversation

To understand Taney's and Lincoln's positions we have to go back to Philadelphia in 1787 and ask how the Framers felt and what they did about slavery.[5] What was their original intent? On one hand there was strong evidence for Taney's view that the Framers of the Constitution wanted to protect slavery. The Framers gave slave states more political protection than they gave free states. They allowed slave states to count three-fifths of their slaves in addition to white people in determining how many Representatives they had. By 1820 this gave the South twenty extra Representatives. The Framers gave slavery economic protection by forbidding taxes on exports, including the export of slave-created products. They said that Congress could not end the international slave trade for twenty years. They provided that fugitive slaves would have to be returned to their masters if they escaped into free states. And the structure of the federal system the Framers created kept the national government from acting directly against slavery. Taney saw all these things. They proved to him that the Constitution clearly and unequivocally protected slavery when it was written.[6]

For Taney that settled the issue and settled it for all time, except for the unlikely event of a constitutional amendment. For Taney insisted that the original intent of the Framers in 1787-1789 compelled obedience. "The Constitution" he said in *Dred Scott*, "must be construed now as it was understood at the time of its adoption . . . . It speaks not only in the same words, but with the same meaning and intent with which it spoke when it came from the hands of its Framers, and was voted on and adopted by the [American] people." And that wasn't just a personal opinion. It was the law of the land. And it was so much the law of the land that nothing could lawfully prevail against it. For the first time in fifty-four years and for only the second time in its history, the Supreme Court struck down a law of the United States Congress. In 1820 Congress had forbade slavery from entering Louisiana Purchase land above 36°30'. But Taney struck down that law. The opinion of the Court trumped the laws of Congress. Further discussion of the issue was foreclosed.

Taney not only asserted primacy, he demanded it. The *Dred Scott* opinion is many things, but one of the most interesting things about its language is how often Taney bangs on the table with phrases like "it is too clear for dispute," "too plain to be misunderstood," "show conclusively," "obviously," "can hardly be supposed," "without doubting for a moment," "too plain to be mistaken," "very clear," "too plain for argument."[7]

One is also struck by Taney's insistence that once racism or pro-slavery opinion can be found in the Framers and their age, it shall and must remain there. His most famous idea from the opinion is probably the statement that the founding generation believed that blacks were an inferior class of beings who "had no rights which the white man was bound to respect." And Taney reinforced that claim by citing laws from Massachusetts and Connecticut as well as federal laws to prove the anti-black racism of the Framers generation. In Taney's world (an old man's world in which many things are fading away) everything is solid and endures. There is no chance that the Framers might have wanted to change or unravel their racism or their commitment to slavery. Those opinions are frozen in the time and place, and we must hold them too for they are "plain, clear, obvious, without doubt, conclusive."

Now another related thing that is striking about this position is that Taney does not ask what the Framers themselves said about their attitude toward slavery. As Harry Jaffa notes, Taney "deduced the meaning of the Fathers' words from what he believed was to be the purport of their actions. He paid no attention to what *they* said about what they meant. He insisted upon *his* understanding of their actions as the sole guide to the meaning of *their* words.[8] Taney thus controlled the past, silencing dissent even from the dead. No objections from the Framers themselves are allowed, no interpretations, no second thoughts or evolving views. In Taney's world no one is doubtful, in conflict, ambiguous, hopeful of change. History does not move in this world, or change or evolve. It, like Taney's Constitution, simply *is*. If slavery was in the Constitution, nothing can change it. The constitutional discussion of the issue, the ongoing conversation about what the document means, is over. "Shut Up!" Taney seems to say "The Court has spoken."

Taney is not a bad man. He was a decent man, a kind and considerate master of slaves, and apparently a gentleman. Justice Samuel F. Miller, appointed by

Roger B. Taney, the fifth Chief Justice of the United States, attempted to settle the slavery controversy in his *Dred Scott* opinion. He argued that the Framers of the Constitution were pro-slavery and that the document must be read that way in perpetuity.

Lincoln, joined Taney's Court prepared to hate him for the *Dred Scott* opinion. But after one Term on the Court Miller reported, "I more than liked him; I loved him."[9] But when it comes to his impact on the Constitution, Taney's good qualities are at least irrelevant. And they may in fact have given him greater power to do the damage he was doing to the constitutional system. Those good qualities may have encouraged him to believe that his good motives guaranteed that good consequences would come from his decisions. They may also have encouraged others to focus on the man's good personal qualities rather than on the harm his ideas were doing. What was wrong about Taney was not his qualities as a human being; what was wrong was his view of the Constitution and of original intent.

But there is another view of the Constitution than Taney's and of the framing that I want to propose and which I think Lincoln believed in too. Whether Lincoln or I thought of it first I'm not sure. I think it is important to note that this other view is not strictly speaking, an alternate view. I'm not saying that the Framers didn't want to protect slavery. I'm saying that they wanted to do some other things too, things that were more important to them than protecting slavery. And that given a choice between the things they wanted to do they probably would have chosen something other than the *Dred Scott* opinion. I believe that Lincoln understood their higher goals, their better original intent.

To understand this point we need to step away from asking what the Framers wanted to do about slavery and ask a larger question, "What was the basic reason they went to Philadelphia in 1787?" (I'm focusing on the Framers in the constitutional convention now although they probably included the ratifiers as Framers too.) They did not go to Philadelphia primarily to protect slavery. They were there to create a new system of government that would overcome the failures of the Articles of Confederation. Slavery was not in danger in 1787, in fact it was safer under the Articles than it would be under any projected national constitution. Had there been a call to organize a new national constitution in order to protect slavery it is doubtful that anyone would have responded.

With the exception of the Deep South delegates, most of the Founding Fathers at Philadelphia, even those from other slave states, didn't like slavery. Madison and Washington and Mason believed slavery to be an evil, as did most of the northern delegates.[10] They didn't protect slavery in the document because they wanted to. They protected it because they had to, because the Deep South delegates threatened to stay out of any government that didn't protect slavery. They knew slavery was the price of the new constitutional union and the total price accumulated ominously.

Yet there were limits on how much protection slavery got. The word never appears in the document—reflecting the fact that the Framers themselves believed slavery an evil and feared that an obvious endorsement of slavery would doom ratification. They carefully avoided suggesting that slavery was lawful except by the municipal law of slave states. They only temporarily accepted the importation of slaves.[11]

What they did positively about slavery they did to protect it in *their* present or their very near future. Even where they allowed the slave trade until 1808 the Framers limited slavery. The Constitution said that the importation of such persons as "any of the States now *existing* shall think proper to admit" couldn't be stopped before 1808.[12] That may suggest that states added after 1787 might not be heard if they wanted to import slaves. While the world of 1787 demanded protection of slavery, there is reason to believe that the Framers had higher hopes for the future.[13] There is reason to believe that the men who wrote slavery into the Constitution were also very critical of it.[14]

Now these critics of slavery were not modern egalitarians. I stress this point because the modern egalitarian standard has been used as an important part of the argument that the Constitution was a proslavery document.[15] Because the people of 1776 and 1787 held racist ideas, the argument goes, they could not have been opposed to slavery. The argument has a long heritage. Taney insisted on that standard in *Dred Scott*. His large catalogue of anti-black legislation in the states during the 1780s prove, to his satisfaction, that equal rights for blacks could never spring from such racist soil and therefore the Framers could not have intended to harm or endanger slavery.[16]

But emphasis on the egalitarian criterion obscures the important ways that the Constitution the Framers created housed potential harms, maybe even disaster, for slavery.

Opposition to slavery does not have to be grounded in faith, in racial equality, or in anger at the injustice it inflicts on slaves. Opposition to slavery can arise just as well because of the belief that slavery is bad for white people. Jefferson, for example, criticized slavery because it allowed masters to become tyrannical brutes.

In the public arena, of course, people can oppose slavery because it threatens the nation and the nation's political constitutional system. They can oppose slavery because it is a menace to the Union and to the possibility of free discussion and debate over goals and options throughout the polity. This was a factor that the members of the Philadelphia convention were viscerally familiar with. The issue of slavery constantly threatened the convention with disruption. In this respect, the convention forecast the later history of slavery and civil liberties and union. It was these dangers, not to the moral climate of the age (though some significant men there had moral concerns), but to the constitutional and social environment that are

Dred Scott sued his master for liberty in 1846 in Missouri, arguing that the four years which Scott had spent in states that banned slavery while his master was an army surgeon had given him freedom. The case spent eleven years in the court system before the Supreme Court decided against Dred Scott in 1857.

the most suggestive for assessing their attitudes toward slavery.

Because their predominant motive was to create a more perfect constitutional system, the Framers saw slavery not as an essential part of that system. They saw it instead as an important factor that had to be quarantined as much as possible to keep it from overthrowing the larger system. The presence of slavery was, as later events would show, potentially profoundly dangerous to the constitutional system as a whole. This was true not only in the sense that it would ultimately challenge the constitutional union itself but also in the sense that it could erode elements of the Constitution that were indispensable to the functioning of the system as a whole.

The Framers certainly knew the dangers that slavery posed. They consciously tried to create a system that would be defended from those dangers. Less consciously, perhaps, they may have also created in the inherent structure of the constitutional system something like a computer virus that attacked as well as defended. For one thing, by creating a constitution that respected the right of a free press and free speech they may have undercut slavery even as they defended it. Consider the relationship between the First Amendment and free speech in the territories. If the amendment, for example, were to be applied to the territories that would mean that Congress, the ultimate law making body for the territories, could not pass laws that interfered with peaceful antislavery agitation. The territories might then become unsafe for slavery. While a pro-slavery Court like Taney's would hardly protect antislavery speech in the territories, Taney was more than eighty and his pro-slavery colleagues were not much younger. A new Court promised new views. Although I can't prove that endangering slavery in the territories by protecting free speech was considered by the Framers, they surely would have recognized the possibility.[17]

But even setting aside this First Amendment threat to slavery, consciously or unconsciously the Framers did, in fact, create a system that endangered slavery. At least that was the opinion of the experts on what threatened slavery in 1861—the eleven seceding states. We also know that the constitutional system had created, by 1860, 1,865,908 voters who gave Lincoln his electoral majority.

Within less than three generations the system created in Philadelphia had brought slavery to this peril. The Framers presumably had a good idea of how that system worked. How far from their conscious intent was the potential for endangering the peculiar institution they had isolated in 1787? We can't know for sure and we can hardly expect to find out by direct testimony from 1787, 1789 or 1791. No framer of the Constitution was going to announce a threat to slavery directly. They wanted slave states to ratify the Constitution. But isn't it reasonable to suppose that given the antislavery feelings of many of them, and their deep understanding of the government they were creating, they foresaw and desired that their government would one day place slavery on the course of extinction?

There are scholars who say that "slavery was an essential component of . . . the American constitutional order."[18] On the contrary slavery was a threat to that very order. Could it reasonably be thought that an institution that limited or killed free speech, free press, petition, assembly, free exercise of religion, (taking only First Amendment rights as a focus), was essential to the constitutional order? Was Congress better off, could it debate, develop thoughtful policies, make better laws with gag rules? Was the constitutional order more vital or viable when slaves could not practice their religion? Was the constitutional order more viable when the correctness, the propriety, the costs of the most explosive issue in the polity could not be discussed in all slave and many free states, in the territories, in Congress? I don't think so. Slavery threatened democratic government, a stable nationhood, the ability of the nation to adapt to changing views of liberty and equality that were sweeping over the western world by the mid nineteenth century. Protecting slavery may have been necessary to get the Constitution in place, but once it was in motion slavery was a threat to its most vital mechanisms and ideals.[19]

By trying to protect it, Taney was like a mad surgeon who operates on a patient threatened by cancer and protects the cancer, shuts down the body's defenses against the disease and then wishes the patient well, after sending him an eight page bill. Taney's constitutional view, resting firmly on his vision of original intent, threatened to destroy the constitutional system the Framers had made.

Lincoln was going to try to discover a meaning for original intent that would preserve and revitalize that system. He certainly knew the necessity of doing so. For it was in the years between 1840 and 1860, when Lincoln began interpreting the Constitution, that the Framers' best hopes and the functioning of their creation were in danger. In those years slavery was repeating in the larger constitutional system its Philadelphia performance—threatening to destroy the system unless its claims were met.

It was in those years that defenders of slavery were shutting down the imperative debate about the greatest danger to the republic. These were the years of the gag rules, the attacks of pro-slavery mobs on abolitionist speakers and writers. These attacks took place not in Dixie's "crowded theater," but in Utica, New York City, Boston, and Alton, Illinois. Not only that, by the late 1850s southern congressmen were pushing for a slave code for the territories where speaking against slavery could be a criminal offense. In this kind of imposed silence was the making of the true "covenant with death."

And the public opinion of these years also contained ominous elements for equal liberty. The so-called rise of the common man under Andrew Jackson in fact saw the meaning of democracy limited to only white men. Blacks, free and slave, and Native Americans saw their rights circumscribed. Foreign born Americans were under attack. And the state legislatures of the land were leading and turning that public opinion into law that reduced especially the rights of free blacks, and cut down on the ability of slaves in the South to be freed by their masters.

Furthermore, all of this was being done in the name of a new vision of slavery. Whereas slavery in the founding years was seen as a necessary evil, it was in these years being defended as a positive good. In 1787 slavery was protected where it existed; seventy years later slavery's reach included places where it could hardly have been imagined years before. Slavery was not a dying institution. It was, thanks in part to Roger B. Taney, with an assist to Stephen Douglas, alive and vital, woven into states and territories, freed from congressional discussion or political debate.[20]

Democracy and the Constitution both entwined with slavery, the fundamental experience of self government and the voice of the Highest Court in the land, both endorsing the right to keep people as property. It was a potent, powerful combination. Lincoln's problem was to overcome it, and offer an alternative vision.

Our modern perspective makes this seem a most formidable task. We believe in judicial supremacy when it comes to interpreting the Constitution. We think of the Court, in Ronald Dworkin's words, as our "Forum of Principle" and accept its decisions as the final word on what the Constitution means; perhaps not always the right word, but almost always the final one.[21]

Lincoln did not live in our world. In Lincoln's age the tradition of judicial supremacy was not yet firmly established. Only twice before the Civil War had the Supreme Court struck down a law of Congress. Only after the Civil War would it begin to do so frequently (eight times in the five years after the Civil War). Thus Lincoln's answer to the constitutional claim of judicial supremacy, on which both Taney and Douglas relied, was to deny it. Of course Lincoln rejected the logic and the theory of the *Dred Scott* opinion. But he also denied that Taney's voice was final. On the contrary, the opinion of the Supreme Court was only part of the larger discussion of what the Constitution meant.

Lincoln denied that the Court was the sole and final interpreter of the meaning of the Constitution. He agreed that the Court's decisions were final for the parties to the particular case decided. And he also agreed that the Court might provide a final statement of what the Constitution meant. But this would be true only after the whole polity had considered the matter at length. If the principle at issue accorded with "the steady practice of the departments throughout our history . . . ," and it had been "before the court more than once, and had there been affirmed and reaffirmed through a course of years, it then might be, perhaps would be, factious, nay, even revolutionary, to not acquiesce in it as a precedent." But the other branches of government retained the obligation to discuss and shape constitutional meanings. Quoting Andrew Jackson (and probably former Attorney General Roger B. Taney), Lincoln said "The Congress, the executive and the court, must each for itself be guided by its own opinion of the Constitution. Each public officer, who takes an oath to support the Constitution, swears that he will support it as he understands it, and not as it is understood by others."[22]

Thus Lincoln insisted Dred Scott's case decided only the fate of Dred Scott; it did not control future congressional legislation on slavery in the territories. Congress, in fact, had a duty to continue to argue and to vote against allowing slavery in the territories. Letting the Supreme Court have the final voice, and hence the power to end discussion of vital and contested issues would mean that "the people will have ceased, to be their own rulers, having to that extent, resigned their government, into the hands of that eminent tribunal."[23]

On vital constitutional issues all branches of government, and the people themselves, were to determine the meaning of the Constitution. The document would be defined by many voices, not one. The voice of the Court had to be transcended, balanced with a wider discussion. A declaration of judicial supremacy, no matter how filled with exclamations of certitude,

Abraham Lincoln greeted supporters at his Springfield home during the 1860 presidential election. Following tradition, he stayed at home prior to the election rather than going out to actively campaign for votes.

could not be the final word. Lawmakers, the President and the people also had to be heard. That was Lincoln's opinion; and possibly also James Madison's. Madison in *Federalist* No. 37 wrote "All new laws, though penned with the greatest technical skill and passed on the fullest and most mature deliberation, are considered as more or less obscure and equivocal, until their meaning be liquidated and ascertained by a series of particular discussions and adjudications." [24] Madison, like Lincoln, seemed to desire an ongoing constitutional conversation.

But expanding the number of voices was only part of Lincoln's task. After all it was Andrew Jackson and Roger B. Taney, both powerful defenders of slavery, who insisted that the Court was not the Constitution's only oracle. Those many voices might simply speak for slavery in the name of "popular sovereignty" or "democracy" or in the name of Taney's Constitution.

Another thing remained to be done and Lincoln would try to do it. Indispensable to a vital constitution was the job of reintroducing into the political/constitutional discourse the ideal of equal liberty that came from the Declaration of Independence.[25] "I have never had a feeling politically," Lincoln once said, "that did not spring from the sentiments embodied in the Declaration of Independence". And throughout the prewar years, and into the war itself perhaps Lincoln's greatest task and accomplishment was to keep the equal liberty of that document alive in the constitutional conversation of the age. "Public sentiment is every thing in this country" he said. "Whoever moulds public sentiment, goes deeper than he who enacts statutes, or pronounces judicial decisions. He makes possible the inforcement of these, else impossible."[26]

Lincoln set out to shape public opinion by showing the nation its best hopes, not its fears. He did not believe, as modern campaign managers often seem to, that people vote their fears. He wanted them to affirm their better angels. He found those angels in the Declaration and in the Constitution.

Now finding them in the Declaration was not an easy task. For even here Taney had placed a roadblock. In the *Dred Scott* opinion the Chief Justice had insisted that the Declaration of Independence was in fact evidence of the Framers pro-slavery views! That little miracle was performed this way: The Founders of the nation, the writers of the Declaration, Taney said, had owned slaves. They were not hypocrites, therefore they did not mean to include black people in the words, "all men are created equal."

To Lincoln, Taney's syllogism proved nothing but the degeneracy of the nation. He was profoundly disturbed about the ways in which the "self evident truth" that "all men are created equal" had become, in the minds of leading Americans like Taney and Stephen Douglas and white Southerners, "a self evident lie." "Near eighty years ago," he said, "we began by declaring that all men are created equal; but now from that beginning we have run down to the other declaration that for SOME men to enslave OTHERS is a sacred right of self government."[27] Lincoln was going to reclaim the Declaration for equality, not slavery.

Now some people worry when a lawyer or judge starts talking about the Declaration of Independence. They fear that person has left the security of legal reasoning and the Constitution and has embraced the vagaries of higher law.[28] Both Taney and Douglas insisted that such rhetoric by Lincoln had cut him loose from the Constitution. They argued that Lincoln was ignoring historical practice and legal precedent in order to advocate his personal radical philosophy. But when Lincoln spoke about the Declaration he was not giving up the Constitution, he was returning it to its ideological roots. For the Framers of the Constitution had lived in the world the revolution created. They had debated the Constitution using the Declaration as a "yardstick." After a book-length study of the *Federalist Papers,* Morton White concludes that the ideology of the Federalist, "was fundamentally the same as the philosophy we find in the Declaration of Independence."[29]

Lincoln therefore legitimately linked the Declaration with the Constitution. If you look through his entire writings, Lincoln never separates the two documents. The men who wrote the two documents, separated in fact by eleven years, are always to Lincoln "the Framers" or "the Founders" engaged in one enterprise, never two. His celebrated Gettysburg Address points to the founding of the nation in 1776 but concludes by resolving that *government* of, by, and for the people "shall not perish from the earth." He was certainly a devotee of the ideals of the Declaration, but he was not choosing the Declaration over the Constitution. He was insisting that the ideals of the Declaration infuse the Constitution and the system founded by the Framers. His critique of slavery targeted not just the rejection of equality; it was replete with criticism that slavery had expanded to corrupt the political dialogue that the Constitution established. What made this intrusion dangerous was that it interfered with the maturing of the ideals of the Declaration, ideals on which the Constitution rested.[30]

Equality in his eyes was not a static concept. Like the Constitution it would attain its fullest meaning over time. In words that may provide the key to understanding Lincoln's ideas on the Constitution and equality, Lincoln said the Framers "meant simply to declare the *right* [to equal liberty], so that enforcement of it might follow as fast as circumstances should permit. They meant to set up a standard maxim for free society, which should be familiar to all, and revered by all: constantly looked to, constantly labored for, and even though never perfectly attained, constantly approximated, and therefore constantly spreading and deepening its influence, and augmenting the happiness and value of life to all people and all colors everywhere."[31]

But the realization of the goal demanded a healthy and open constitutional system in which the meanings of equality might be debated, voted on, chosen, tested. And slavery, as it had in Philadelphia in 1787, threatened that open discussion, stifled that testing. Lincoln therefore not only spoke for equality, he spoke for an open constitutional system, an ongoing constitutional conversation. Throughout the 1850s and into 1860 Lincoln's critique emphasized the importance of an ongoing debate about slavery and equality. And he challenged any effort to still that debate.

He challenged *Dred Scott* as shutting down discussion of equality as a political principle. He also worried that *Dred Scott* might be followed by a Court decision that would shut down discussion of slavery even in the free states. As the election of 1860 approached, Lincoln also criticized the South for not letting Republicans campaign in the southern states. And of course ultimately he would deny to Dixie the right to abandon the electoral process in service of the peculiar institution. Lincoln had a powerful devotion to the political/constitutional conversation set up by the Framers.[32]

Taney's history and his Constitution were frozen in time, a time when Framers wrote racist laws and thus built an inescapable pro-slavery Constitution that abided unchanged forever, enslaving blacks and whites for as long as the Constitution endured. Taney's constitution was on a collision course with the history that lay before the nation. He endorsed a constitution based on what the Framers had feared and held it paralyzed within that fear.

When Taney looked at original intent he saw the Constitution as a structure, a system of rules set down in the past which must be followed faithfully by all succeeding generations. But Lincoln had a different view of what it was. He thought that it was a process, a conversation, not a proclamation; an instrument, not an incantation. The Constitution was what the Constitution did, as much or more than what the Constitution said. This does not mean for a moment that Lincoln thought that you could reject or ignore the Constitution when new demands or new situations made it unwieldy. It means that the Constitution itself set up the means whereby it could respond to new ideas, meet new situations, as well as call people back to contemplate its original ideals and meanings. Both Taney and Lincoln respected the original intent of the Framers. Taney admired what they had established; Lincoln treasured what they had set in motion.[33]

Lincoln's vision was of a history in which the Framers had wanted to realize their best hopes and fulfill what Lincoln might later call "the better angels of our nature." They set up a constitutional system to do that, one which would maintain and confirm and demand an abiding conversation about constitutional meaning and ideals. And slavery had challenged that conversation, endangering the means as well as the ends of the ongoing discussion. Taney had wanted that conversation to end. Lincoln insisted that it continue into an unending and progressive future. He saw slavery's challenge to the nation not only as a challenge to ideals, but as a menace to the constitutional process.

As an adult Lincoln had two callings: lawyer and politician. Both occupations made him profoundly committed to the rule of law and the Constitution. From his first speeches in the late 1830s to his decision in 1861 to accept war to preserve the political constitutional system established by the Constitution, Lincoln demonstrated that commitment. But he also recognized that system had an ideological heritage born also in the late eighteenth century—the idea of equal liberty under law. By insisting on the inherent, inescapable, interrelationship between the Constitution's process and the Declaration's ideals he helped keep both the nation's means and ends alive, the better to "secure the blessings of liberty," as the preamble said, "to ourselves and our posterity."

Endnotes

[*] This essay is a revised version of "Hercules Unbound: Lincoln, Slavery and the Intentions of the Framers," in ***The Constittuion, Law, and American Life: Critical Aspects of the Nineteenth Century Experience***, Donald Nieman, ed. (Athens University of Georgia, 1992).

[1] William M. Wiecek, "The Witch at the Christening: Slavery and the Constitution's Origins," in ***The Framing and Ratification of the Constitution***, Leonard Levey and Dennis Mahomy, eds. (New York: Macmillian, 1987), 167.

[2] William M. Wiecek, "Slavery and Abolition Before the United States Supreme Court," 65 ***Journal of American History*** 35-56 (1978); Edward S. Corwin, "The Dred Scott Decision in the Light of Contemporary Legal Doctrines," 17 ***American Historical Review*** 52-69 (1911). Harry Jaffa, ***Crisis of the House Divided*** (Chicago, 1982. First published, Seattle: University of Washington, 1959). Douglas in Roy P. Basler et al., eds. ***The Collected Works of Abraham Lincoln*** (9 vols., New Brunswick: Rutgers University Press, 1953-55) III, 142-143, 243. Wiecek comments in his article that "If war is too serious to be entrusted to the military, at times the American constitution is too serious to be entrusted to the judges." He makes the comment to suggest the disastrous effects of judicial constitution-making in *Dred Scott*. It is the burden of the present article to show how one might entrust the Constitution to extrajudicial arenas.

[3] Goethe, ***Campaign in France***, July 25, 1793.

[4] Thurgood Marshall, "The Constitution's Bicentennial: Commemorating the Wrong Document?," 40 ***Vanderbilt Law Review*** 1337-1342 (1987).

[5] I follow Donald Robinson's ***Slavery in the Structure of American Politics, 1765-1820*** (New York: Harcourt, Brace, 1971) in describing what the Framers did about slavery, but believe that in writing about the subject of slavery in the constitutional system he has naturally enough overemphasized the role of slavery at Philadelphia in 1787.

[6] William M. Wiecek and Paul Finkelman both point to the two clauses in the Constitution which promised military support to put down domestic violence and to suppress insurrections as designed to protect slavery. Robinson argues that slavery's supporters felt able to put down their own uprisings and would have worried about sending Massachusetts militia into Dixie even for this purpose. Paul Finkelman, "Slavery and the Constitutional Convention: Making a Covenant with Death" in ***Beyond Confederation: Origins of the Constitution and American National Identity***, Richard Beeman, ed. (Chapel Hill: University of North Carolina, 1987), 191-2; William M. Wiecek, ***The Sources of Antislavery Constitutionalism in America, 1760-1848***, (Ithaca: Cornell University Press, 1977), 62-63. Robinson, *Supra* n. 3 at 218n. Robinson notes that southern delegates usually wanted to limit the extent of these provisions.

[7] 60 U.S. (19 How.) 410-426 (1857).

[8] Harry Jaffa, with Bruce Ledewitz, Robert L. Stone, George Anastaplo ***Original Intent and the Framers of the Constitution: A Disputed Question*** (Washington, D.C.: Regnery Gateway, 1994), 29.

[9] Miller quoted in G. Edward White, ***The American Judicial Tradition*** (New York: Oxford University Press, 1976), 66-7.

[10] *See* articles by William Freehling, "The Founding Fathers and Slavery," 77 ***American Historical Review*** 81 (1972); Don E. Fehrenbacher, "Slavery, the Framers, and the Living Constitution," in ***Slavery and Its, Consequences: The Constitution, Equality and Race***, Robert Goldwin and Art Kaufman, eds. (Washington, D.C.: American Enterprise Institute, 1988), 1-22, and articles by Herbert Storing and W.B. Allen in this latter collection for most recent views of antislavery intention of the founders.

[11] Herbert Storing, "Slavery and the Moral Foundations of the American Republic," in ***Slavery and Its Consequences***, Goldwin and Kaufman, eds. 53-54.

[12] Don Fehrenbacher, "Slavery the Framers and the Living Constitution", in ***Slavery and Its Consequences***, Goldwin and Kaufman, eds. 9-10.

[13] Robinson, ***Slavery in the Structure of American Politics, 1765-1820***, 227-228. Some at the convention apparently believed that slavery and the slave trade might be dying. *See* p. 225.

[14] One scholar writing about the Constitutional Convention notes that "Slavery had been confined to a cul-de-sac, where it would be virtually unnecessary, as it would surely be impolitic, for national politicians to handle it." Robinson, *supra* n. 3, at 244.

[15] *See* William Wiecek, "'The Blessings of Liberty': Slavery in the American Constitutional Order," in ***Slavery and Its Consequences: The Constitution, Equality, and Race***, Robert Goldwin and Art Kaufman, eds. (Washington, D.C.: American Enterprise Institute, 1988), 24-29; Finkelman, "Slavery and the Constitutional Convention: Making A Covenant with Death" in ***Beyond Confederation***, 223-224.

[16] 60 U.S. (19 How.) 410-417 (1857).

[17] I asked members of a panel at the 1988 Southern Historical Association, Peter Onuf, Robert Weir, John

Murrin, and Richard Beeman, if they had knowledge of contemporary discussions of applying the Bill of Rights to the territories and they said that they had no such information. But note that Taney himself in *Dred Scott* at 60 U.S. (19 How.), at 450 argues that the Bill of Rights would stop Congress from abridging free speech and press and petition as well as the other provisions of the Bill in the territories.

[18] Wiecek, "The Blessings of Liberty" in ***Slavery and Its Consequences***, Goldwin and Kaufman, eds., pp. 24-29.

[19] W.B. Allen, "A New Birth of Freedom: Fulfillment or Derailment?" in ***Slavery and Its Consequences***, Goldwin and Kaufman, eds., 89-90, note 3. Paul Brest, "The Misconceived Quest for the Original Understanding," 60 ***Boston University Law Review*** 226 (1980).

[20] Fehrenbacher, "Slavery, the Framers, and the Living Constitution," ***Slavery and Its Consequences***, Goldwin and Kaufman, eds., 1-22. William M. Wiecek, in "Slavery and Abolition Before the United States Supreme Court," 65 ***Journal of American History*** 34-56 (1978); Edward S. Corwin "The Dred Scott Decision in the Light of Contemporary Legal Doctrines," 17 ***American Historical Review*** 52-69 (1911). Harry Jaffa, ***Crisis of the House Divided*** (Chicago, 1982. First published, Seattle: University of Washington, 1959). Douglas in ***Collected Works of Abraham Lincoln***, III, 142-143, 243.

[21] Ronald Dworkin, "The Forum of Principle," 56 ***New York University Law Review*** 469-518 (1981).

[22] ***Collected Works of Abraham Lincoln***, II, 400-403. I follow two excellent essays on Lincoln's ideas of judicial review: John Agresto, "The Limits of Judicial Supremacy: A Proposal for 'Checked Activism,'" 14 ***Georgia Law Review*** 471-495 (1980); and Gary Jacobsohn, "Abraham Lincoln 'On This Question of Judicial Authority': The Theory of Constitutional Aspiration," 36 ***Western Political Quarterly***, 52-70 (1983).

[23] ***Collected Works of Abraham Lincoln***, II, 495; IV, 268.

[24] Jacob E. Cooke, ed., ***The Federalist*** 236. (Middletown, CT: Wesleyan University Press, 1961).

[25] Harry Jaffa, ***Crisis of the House Divided***, Chapter 17 notes the contradiction inherent in affirming popular consent while denying equality. The concept of consent rests on the belief that government legitimately rests on equal individuals whose opinions must be consulted. The escape of the Court and of Douglas was of course to deny that blacks and whites could be equal, and to insist that all white men, but not black, were created equal and hence provided the necessary consent to government.

[26] ***Collected Works of Abraham Lincoln***, IV, 240 and II, 552-553.

[27] ***Collected Work of Abraham Lincoln***, II, 275.

[28] Phillip Paludan, "Lincoln, the Rule of Law, and the American Revolution," 70 ***Journal of the Illinois State Historical Society***, 10-18 (1977); Paludan, "Lincoln and the Rhetoric of Politics," ***Presidents, Politics and People: American Politics in the Civil War Era***, Lloyd Ambrosius, ed. (Lincoln, U. of Nebraska, forthcoming, 1989) Mark Neely summarizes the historical view that Lincoln was a proponent of the Declaration "rather than" the Constitution. ***The Abraham Lincoln Encyclopedia***, 70. Harry Jaffa contrasts Douglas' position on the side of the Constitution against Lincoln's defense of the Declaration. *See* ***Crisis of the House***, Chapter 15. Although Gary Jacobsohn argues that Lincoln had an aspirational view of the Constitution he still seems to separate the Declaration from the Constitution by neglecting to demonstrate the interaction between the two documents. *See* "Abraham Lincoln 'On This Question of Judicial Authority'," *supra*, note 20.

[29] Frederick R. Black, "The American Revolution as 'Yardstick' in the Debates on the Constitution, 1787-1788," 117 ***Proceedings of the American Philosophical Society***, 162-185 (1973); describes the many ways in which the meaning of the Constitution of 1787 was connected to the events and experiences of 1776. There is a whole historiography discussing whether the Articles of Confederation or the Constitution best represents the Declaration's goals. Those contending that the Constitution fulfills the Declaration include Clinton Rossiter, ***1787: The Grand Convention*** (New York: MacMillan, 1966); Benjamin F. Wright, ***Consensus and Continuity, 1776-1787*** (Boston: Boston University Press, 1958); Robert Brown, ***Charles Beard and the Constitution*** (Princeton: Princeton University Press, 1956); Edmund Morgan, ***The Birth of the Republic*** (Chicago: University of Chicago Press, 1956); and Esmond Wright, ***Fabric of Freedom: 1763-1800*** (New York: Hill and Wang, 1961). Hannah Arendt in ***On Revolution***, sees the Constitution as providing the power to the nation to achieve the goals of 1776. Supporters of the Articles include Merrill Jensen, ***The Articles of Confederation*** (Madison: University of Wisconsin Press, 1940); and Jackson T. Main, ***The AntiFederalists: Critics of the Constitution 1781-1788*** (Chapel Hill: University of North Carolina Press, 1961). Gordon Wood notes how the Federalists appropriated the words and phrases of the Revolution to achieve less democratic ends. The overall point here is that 1776 and 1787 were integrated in the minds of the Framers in many ways. Also relevant is work connecting the Declaration and the Constitution as coherent parts of the same philosophy. *See* Martin Diamond, "The Declaration and the Constitution: Liberty, Democracy and the Founders," 41 ***Public Interest*** 39-55 (1975); Morton White, ***Philosophy, "The Federalist," and the Constitu-***

tion (New York, Oxford University Press, 1987), 226. Leonard Levy observes that "One has only to read the state recommendations for a bill of rights to know that the natural rights philosophy seized the minds of the Framers as it had the minds of the rebellious patriots of 1776." ***Original Intent and the Framers' Constitution*** (New York: MacMillan, 1988), 279.

[30] ***Collected Works of Abraham Lincoln***, IV, 240; W.B. Allen, "A New Birth of Freedom: Fulfillment or Derailment?" in ***Slavery and Its Consequences***, 66.

[31] ***Collected Works of Abraham Lincoln*** II, 406; W.B. Allen, *supra*, note 27, refers to this point in a similar way, "The dynamics of democracy," he writes, "more than any direct provisions of the Constitution, were the source of the antislavery implications of the founding. In that way the political accomplishment of the Constitution of 1787 was to deepen the influence and authority of the Declaration of Independence."

[32] ***Collected Works of Abraham Lincoln***, III, 535-550. Lincoln claimed that the *Dred Scott* decision would be followed by a decision protecting the rights of slave owners in the states. Historians have discovered a pending case in New York which might have done just that. *See Lemmon v. People*, 20 N.Y. (6 Smith) 562 (1860); Paul Finkelman, "The Nationalization of Slavery: A Counter-factual Approach to the 1860s," ***Louisiana Studies***, (1975), 213-240; Harold Hyman and William Wiecek, ***Equal Justice Under Law***, (New York: Harper & Row, 1982); 192-196. The latter authors provide much evidence to undercut their claim that Lincoln's assertion that the Supreme Court might protect slavery even within free states deserved to be taken seriously. For example, the New York courts rejected the argument of counsel for slave owners that the privileges and immunities clause of the Constitution protected sojourning slave owners in New York. The New York State legislature wrote a resolution declaring that "this state will not allow slavery within her borders, in any form, under any pretence, or for any time however short." Massachusetts, Ohio, Maine, Vermont and Pennsylvania all passed similar laws. In the aftermath of the reaction to *Dred Scott* would Taney's Court have been that bold again? *See* Don Fehrenbacher, ***The Dred Scott Case*** (New York: Oxford University Press, 1978), 432-5. I mention the *Lemmon* case to admit the logic of Lincoln's views, expressed at Galesburg, that the Constitution as shaped by the logic of the Taney position might house expanded protections for slavery. *See* ***Collected Works of Abraham Lincoln***, III, 230-234 (Oct. 7, 1858). Note the difference in time here. Lincoln was over a year and a half ahead of the *Lemmon* case in making his observation.

[33] There are several reasons to agree with Lincoln, for the Constitution sets up a series of conversations which require and nurture responses to changing events and ideas. Within each house of Congress legislators must debate and reason together. The Congress also negotiates with the President and vice versa. Both the President and Congress must engage the public in conversation about means and ends. The Constitution requires elections every two years. The Supreme Court is part of this constitutional conversation, comparing what Congress and the president and then the state governments have done with the Constitution. It then speaks its piece and Congress and the states and the people can respond within the political and legal process. I think that if you want to see the world in which the Constitution was supposed to operate you need to look at the First Amendment which envisions a free press, free speech, people petitioning the governments, assembling to discuss and debate options, a society gathered in a great political constitutional conversation. Lincoln, the great conversationalist, the great lawyer and the great politician felt this Constitution in his very bones. And he felt that slavery threatened that Constitution profoundly and other people shared his concern. For fuller discussion of the use of the conversation metaphor in analyzing the Constitution *see* my "Lincoln and the Rhetoric of Politics" in ***Crisis of Republicanism***, Lloyd Ambrosius, ed. (Lincoln: University of Nebraska Press, 1990), 73-93; Sotirios Barber, ***On What the Constitution Means*** (Baltimore: Johns Hopkins University Press, 1984); James Boyd White, ***When Words Lose Their Meaning: Constitutions and Reconstitutions of Language, Character, and Community*** (Chicago: University of Chicago Press, 1984).

Salmon Portland Chase and the Judicial Culture of the Supreme Court in the Civil War Era

G. Edward White

Salmon P. Chase is one of the least well known of the small number of individuals who have served as Chief Justice of the United States. The history of the Supreme Court is often telescoped into the succession of Chief Justices that symbolize the continuity of the institution, and some Chiefs have been assigned leading roles in that history. In a popularized version, John Marshall and Roger B. Taney are singled out in the nineteenth century, and then there is a hiatus until the appearance of the next Chief Justice of genuine importance, Charles Evans Hughes in the 1930s. Chase, who was Chief for only nine years, is assigned to the obscure group of men who led the Court between the Civil War and the Depression. Moreover, in the popular historical imagination Chase is a remote and inaccessible figure. To the extent that much is known about him, he is thought of as a judge who would have been more effective in his office had he not been possessed of apparently insatiable political ambitions. Chase's jurisprudence, when discussed, has tended to be dismissed as arcane.

Salmon P. Chase was the sixth Chief Justice of the United States. Appointed by President Lincoln in 1864 he served until his death in 1873.

I believe that Chase's historical reputation has been undervalued, and this essay seeks to present some information that might be helpful in forging a revisionist account of his career as Chief Justice. I have written elsewhere on Chase's constitutional jurisprudence;[1] this essay focuses on the internal judicial culture of the Supreme Court during Chase's tenure as Chief Justice. By judicial culture I mean not only the Court's internal deliberative process, but the attitudes about law and judging, and about the relationship of the Court to external events in American society, revealed by that process.

The image of Chase as a relative nonentity contrasts sharply with the appraisal of him by contemporaries when he became Chief Justice. Abraham

Lincoln, who appointed him, said he was "about one and a half times bigger than any other man I ever knew." Justice Samuel Miller, not given to favorable judgments of his colleagues, said he knew "of no one against whom I should undertake to measure myself with more diffidence than Chase." Such comments were often accompanied by another, related appraisal of Chase. That appraisal centered on his ambition, and his tendency to give others the impression that he was meeting them and conversing with them on a path to going somewhere else. As Rutherford B. Hayes put it, "political intrigue, love of power and boundless ambition were the striking features of his life and character." David Davis, who also served with Chase on the Court, wrote in 1870 that "Chase is the most ambitious man, except [Stephen] Douglas, that I ever knew personally." Miller notwithstanding his earlier remarks on Chase, said that his strengths were "warped, perverted and shrivelled by the selfishness generated by ambition."[2]

There is no question that Chase liked some features of the job of Chief Justice far better than others. Supreme Court jurisdiction in the Chase period was noticeably different from what it is now. The Justices currently have the luxury of primarily setting their own docket through discretionary use of their power to hear or decline to hear petitions for certiorari from lower federal and state courts. They might not agree with a characterization of the certiorari process as a "luxury," but the process is surely more selective than that of Chase's time, when the Court's jurisdiction included direct appeals, limited only by diversity of citizenship and modest jurisdictional monetary amounts, from nonconstitutional as well as constitutional cases decided in the lower federal courts. A large number of cases on the Court's docket while Chase was Chief Justice involved issues such as land title disputes in Kentucky or Tennessee where an out-of-state resident and an in-state squatter vied over the title. Shortly after his appointment Chase described his new job, in a diary entry in 1864, as "[w]orking from morning till midnight, and no result, except that John Smith owned this parcel of land or other property instead of Jacob Robinson; I caring nothing, and nobody caring much more, about the matter."[3]

Chase may not have cared about the substance of many of the cases that came before him as Chief Justice, but he cared a good deal about the setting and structure in which the Court decided cases, and particularly about relieving the Justices from some of the routine and trivial features of their job. Like his predecessors Marshall and Taney, he realized that special opportunities existed for the Chief Justice in the management of the Court's docket and the structuring of its internal process of decisionmaking, and he sought to take advantage of those opportunities.

Justice Samuel F. Miller served with Chief Justice Salmon Portland Chase for nine years. Chase called Miller "the dominant personality . . . upon the bench, whose mental force and individuality are felt by the Court more than any other."

Let me begin this discussion of Chase's response to the Court's judicial culture during his tenure by noting a few features of that culture. First was the composition of the Court itself. During 1864 and 1873, the years of Chase's tenure, the number of Justices on the Court fluctuated significantly. Congress, mindful of the expanding territorial reach of the American continent and the growing amount of litigation generated by demographic and territorial expansion, resolved to expand the circuits in which lower federal courts were grouped. By the time of Chase's appointment there were ten Circuits, and

Chase was the tenth Justice on a ten-member Court. But after the Civil War ended, the Reconstruction Congress, infuriated with President Andrew Johnson, declared its intention to reduce the size of the Court to six in an 1866 statute. This resulted in the Court's size being reduced through attrition in the next three years. In 1865, Justice Catron died and the Court went from ten Justices to nine; in 1867, Justice James Moore Wayne died and the Court went from nine Justices to eight; and in 1870, Justice Robert Grier resigned and the Court went from eight Justices to seven. By then Johnson had been succeeded by Ulysses S. Grant as President and Congress had relented, expanding the size of the Court to nine Justices in an 1869 statute and allowing Grant to name two additional Justices. Needless to say, the size of the Court was a matter of tactical importance, because if there were eight Justices or ten, as was the case for some of Chase's tenure, equally divided votes in cases were possible, a result that automatically affirmed the judgment of the lower court from which the case had come.

Another important feature of the job of Supreme Court Justice during Chase's tenure was circuit riding. Circuit riding was, of course, literally riding on horseback, or by other conveyance, around the country to hold court in various locations. The staffing of the federal courts through the period of Chase's Chief Justiceship was such that there were no intermediate courts of appeal. Instead, there was a court designated as a circuit court, but actually composed of two judges from other courts, the Supreme Court Justice assigned to the particular federal circuit and the district judge of the area where the courthouse was located. Together they formed the circuit court. The circuit courts met irregularly, their opening for business coinciding with the times when a Supreme Court Justice assigned to a particular circuit, having finished his duties in Washington, would ride down to a particular locality and hold court.

This time investment of Supreme Court Justices in circuit riding was very considerable. The Justices rode twice a year, in the spring and the fall. During the tenures of Marshall and Taney the Supreme Court's Term in Washington had only lasted six to eight weeks, beginning in the middle of January or early February and ending by the middle of March. The rest of the time the Justices were either at home or riding the circuit. By Chase's tenure, the expansion of territory and of federal circuits combined with the extant jurisdiction of the Court to create what might be called a mini-crisis for the Court's docket.

That docket increased dramatically, leading Chase to take the first steps toward creating the modern Supreme Court's calendar. He lengthened the time in which the Justices remained in Washington, first, between 1864 and 1867, from fourteen to seventeen weeks, and then from 1868 to his death in 1873, from seventeen to thirty weeks. Chase did this by creating the "adjourned Term," in which the Court continued to sit in Washington after hearing all the cases before it in the spring Term. During the adjourned Term the Justices rarely heard additional cases, but disposed of the backlog of cases, deciding which ones would continue on their docket and resolving some cases they had not rendered opinions on in the past spring Term. And by 1873, the year of Chase's death, the Court institutionalized his adjourned Term practice by formally extending its Term to the first Monday in October; thereafter Terms ran from October through late spring.

During Chase's tenure he was also very active, if not entirely successful, in securing Congressional legislation to alleviate the Court's workload. He or one of his judicial colleagues regularly drafted suggested legislation proposing a reform of the Supreme Court's operations, but Congress was never willing fully to endorse it. A major component of the suggested legislation was a proposal to create circuit courts of appeal. This would not only have relieved the Justices' workload, but would also made it possible to eliminate circuit riding. In 1869 Congress responded partially to the workload issue by creating new circuit judgeships, thereby adding a sitting judge for each of the circuits. But it balked on eliminating circuit riding or the obligation of Supreme Court Justices to serve as circuit judges. Many members of Congress believed that circuit riding was the Court's primary connection to the special circumstances local lawyers faced across the nation. Since certiorari did not yet exist, circuit court work required Justices to continue to deal with the various technicalities and orientations of local law. This dimension of the Court's work helps explain the geographic bias of Supreme Court appointments, which lasted until this century. When a Justice retired from a particular region, a nominating President felt pressure from Congress to appoint another Justice from that region. There is no comparable pressure today, in large part because there is no circuit riding. But during Chase's tenure the first two appointments that Congress permitted Grant to make in 1870 were decisively affected by regional considerations. Circuit riding, despite Chase's efforts, was not abolished until 1891.

Another dimension of the Court's judicial culture during Chase's tenure was the distinctive process by which the Justices deliberated cases. One element of that process was the considerable weight attached to oral argument. In Chase's day there was a limit of two counsel per side with a time limitation of two hours each; in effect this meant a minimum of four hours for each litigant. Thus Chase and his fellow Justices spent a great deal of time in Court, listening to oral arguments. They did not spend nearly as much time reading briefs, because nothing like modern briefs were filed. Instead, lawyers arguing before the Court filed a "summary of points" before their arguments commenced; the summary merely introduced the Justices to the material an advocate would cover in his presentation.

After the completion of arguments the Justices repaired to their consultation room, which was adjacent to the room in the basement of the Capitol that served as the Supreme Court's courtroom. In Marshall's day there had not even been a consultation room in the Capitol; the Justices had held their deliberations in a boarding house, where they lived during the short time they stayed in Washington. As Justice Joseph Story reported, the informality of the boarding house setting during Marshall's tenure provided the Justices an opportunity for ongoing dialogue about the cases, which resulted in decisions being rendered strikingly close to the time they had been argued. By Chase's time, however, there was a consultation room, the Justices no longer lived together in a boarding house, and the process of decision making had become more formal. Justice John A. Campbell gave an account of the conferences in a period just before Chase's tenure which can be taken as closely mirroring those held in the time of Chase. "The Chief Justice usually called the case," Campbell wrote. "[H]e stated the pleadings and the facts that they presented, the arguments and his conclusions in regard to them. Then the question was put whether the judgment or decrees should be reversed and each Justice according to his precedent [seniority] commencing with the junior Justice was regarded to his judgment and his reasons for his conclusion. The concurring opinions of the majority decided the cause and signified the opinion to be given."[4]

The process Campbell described constituted an interesting variation on what is taken to be the Court's current process in conference, where the Justices speak in turn formally and in order of seniority, beginning with the Chief Justice, but then vote in reverse order of seniority. In Chase's day, once the Chief Justice had introduced the case, the junior Justice spoke first and stated how he was prepared to vote and why, with the remaining Justices then speaking in terms of ascending seniority. Under the current practice, after votes have been tallied at Conference, an assignment of the majority opinion is made, typically by the Chief Justice or the senior Associate Justice if the Chief is not with the majority, and the designated Justice writes a draft of the opinion. That Justice then circulates that draft to the other members of the majority, who signify their assent to it or make comments and suggestions for revision. In the current Court majority opinion writing is a collaborative process, with many Justices having some input into the formal majority opinion that ends up being printed in the *U.S. Reports*.

In Chase's Court there is no evidence that this collaboration on written draft opinions occurred. As Campbell put it, "the concurring opinions of the majority. . . signified the opinion to be given." That "opinion," called "the opinion of the Court," was assigned by the Chief Justice to himself or to another Justice, but that Justice's "opinion" was delivered orally in Court. There was no draft circulation, no give and take, so that the opinion essentially reflected only the views of the individual person to whom the opinion was assigned. After the opinion was read in Court, it was sent to the Court's Reporter, who would edit it and publish it in the *U.S. Reports*. None of the other Justices voting in the majority had participated beyond their discussion of the case in conference. Indeed, the configuration of votes in most cases is unknown for the Chase era, since Justices who voted against the result endorsed by the majority opinion often acquiesced silently in that

As Chief Justice, Roger B. Taney exerted considerable control over the assignment of opinions during his tenure, though he was less successful than his predecessor, Chief Justice John Marshall, in squelching dissenting opinions.

result. Nor did "opinions of the Court" typically reveal whether they represented the views of all the Justices or a bare majority. As a result it was very hard to tell how divided the Court was on certain issues.

The relative informality and unaccountability of the Chase Court's internal deliberative process, at least when compared with twentieth-century Courts, suggests that Chase had considerable opportunities to exert influence with his colleagues through his prerogatives of framing cases and assigning opinions. But there is no strong evidence that Chase was conspicuously successful in using those powers to his advantage. Chief Justice Marshall, for example, had taken advantage of his seniority prerogatives and intellectual powers to assign many important opinions to himself and to discourage his fellow Justices from writing concurrences or dissents. Chief Justice Taney likewise controlled the assignment process during his tenure, but was somewhat less inclined to discourage dissenting opinions. He drew the line, however, at circulating "opinions of the Court" to prospective dissenters. In the *Dred Scott* case, after considerable internal skirmishing, Taney issued an opinion that was designated the "opinion of the Court," but delayed in releasing it to the Reporter for publication. Justice Benjamin R. Curtis, anxious to publish his dissent, requested and managed to obtain a draft of Taney's opinion. To Taney's great consternation, Curtis then responded directly to many of the points in the Taney opinion in his dissent, and published the dissent independently in Boston prior to the official publication of the majority opinion on Washington. Taney was enraged and accused Curtis of publishing his dissent in an effort to inflame public opinion against the decision of the Court. The incident seemed to reinforce the established view that open publication of dissenting opinions should be discouraged.

If that norm was still controlling when Chase succeeded Taney as Chief Justice, there is no strong evidence that Chase was particularly effective in enforcing it. More published dissents and concurrences appeared during Chase's tenure than had surfaced in previous eras, although a large number of cases were decided without any concurrences or dissents. But we cannot use modern standards to infer from this that Chase was an effective or ineffective internal strategist, since the Court's deliberative process itself discouraged the writing of separate opinions.

We can, however, glean something about Chase's interest in using his prerogatives as Chief Justice to further his own jurisprudential agenda, and also something about his conventional image as an ambitious "politician," from one episode in his judicial career. That episode involved the two celebrated cases, *Hepburn v. Griswold* (1870) and *The Legal Tender Cases* (1871), in which the Chase Court first invalidated, and then upheld, the constitutionality of federally-issued "greenback" paper money as legal tender. The second of the decisions was made by an enlarged nine-man Court, both of whose new members voted to permit greenbacks as legal tender, a position endorsed by President Grant, who had appointed them, and vigorously opposed by Chase.

Although Chase had actually been responsible for the issuance of federal paper currency, a measure he instituted as Secretary of the Treasury under Lincoln during the Civil War, he was strongly wedded to the conceptual premise that all currency other than gold

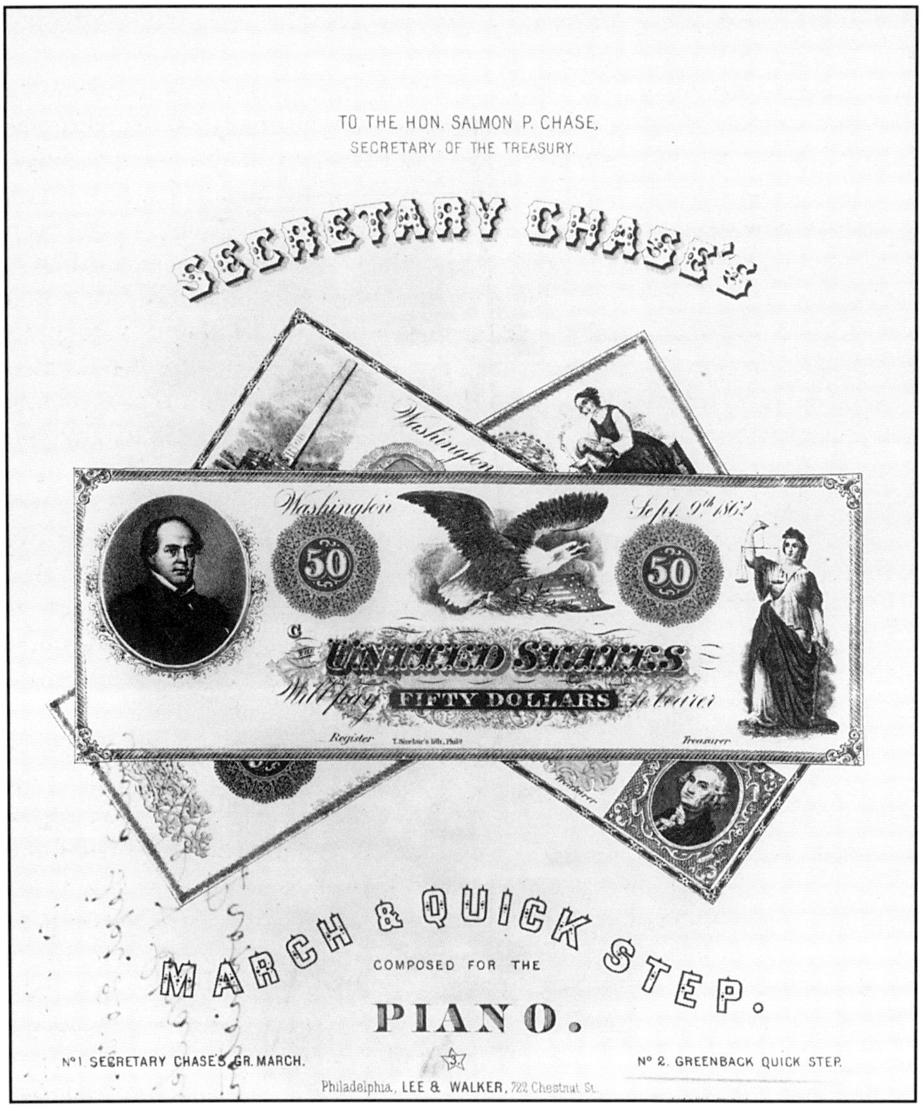

While Secretary of the Treasury, Salmon P. Chase instituted the issuance of federal paper currency. However, as Chief Justice of the United States, Chase ruled that paper money had "no intrinsic value."

and silver coin ("specie") was inherently unstable and should not be made legal tender for the payment of debts. Congress, however, issued a statute in 1862 authorizing the issuance of federal bank notes and making them legal tender for public and private debts, and Chase, as Secretary of the Treasury, was charged with raising money for the northern war effort. He proposed to borrow coin from banking institutions, and then use that coin reserve to back up the new national paper currency. His plan, as explained by one of his contemporary biographers, J. W. Shuckers, was to "supply a sound and uniform currency" by following three steps. "First, a circulation of notes bearing a common impression and authenticated by a common authority (that of a national Government); second, the redemption of these notes by the associations and institutions to which they were to be delivered for issue; and third, the security of that redemption by the pledge of United States stocks, and an adequate provision of specie."[5]

The banking community balked at Chase's plan. They informed Chase that they would loan the U.S. Treasury money, beginning with an initial loan of $50 million dollars, but they could not guarantee to pay individuals redeeming greenbacks in any specific currency. Instead, they would pay the bearer of a greenback in the currency that was requested for payment, be it state bank notes or any other currency. This was to ensure that the banks did not deplete their own reserves of coin. Chase rejected the offer, insisting that when a bank dealt with the U.S. government, all obligations had to be paid out in coin. The response from the bankers was that there would be no loans beyond the $50 million they had agreed to loan the government, as they would have no hard currency left on which to base further loans

Chase countered by proposing that all state bank currency be withdrawn and replaced with U.S. currency. While matters remained at an impasse, "greenbacks" continued in circulation, people contracted debts, and greenbacks were used to pay off those debts. At the same time the value of greenbacks fluctuated wildly, and loan repayment with greenbacks became a hazardous enterprise.

Eventually one citizen of Kentucky sued another over a promissory note made before the passage of the 1862 statute authorizing federal paper money. The creditor insisted on payment in specie, and the Supreme Court of Kentucky agreed, holding the statute unconstitutional. The debtor appealed on a writ of error to the Chase Court. Chase's opinion for the Court upheld the Kentucky court's ruling, and Chase was personally invested in the result. As his opinion in *Hepburn v. Griswold*, the first of the legal tender cases, noted, paper currency had "no intrinsic value, but a purchasing value," whereas coin currency had "intrinsic value, determined by the weight and fitness of the metal."[6]

In an age in which plastic cards are treated as the equivalent of specie, it may be difficult to reconstruct the assumption that coin retains a kind of permanence, but no other form of currency does. Chase's view, however, was not idiosyncratic. It was widely shared by many nineteenth century economic theorists: Chase had formed his views on political economy when he was a young lawyer in Ohio in the 1830s. Despite his willingness to issue greenbacks while he was Secretary of the Treasury, Chase was convinced that the only sound policy was to have the payment of debts in coin required as legal tender. He did not take this position because of its political implications; he adopted it because he believed it was "sound" and thus morally right. But he was not able to convince all of his fellow Justices that the Legal Tender Act of 1862 was "unsound" and thus unconstitutional. He was only able to convince a bare majority, which included the mentally failing Justice Robert Grier, that the statute was unconstitutional when applied to debts contracted before its passage.

Indeed Grier's vote itself was shaky. *Hepburn v. Griswold* had been combined with a second case involving a promissory note in a different jurisdiction, and the two cases had been heard simultaneously by the Court. When the Justices met in conference, Justice Grier voted in *Hepburn* against the constitutionality of making greenbacks legal tender, but in the other case he voted for it. He was reminded by his brethren that the votes were perhaps inconsistent, and after further discussion, it appeared that Justice Grier believed that the 1862 statute could be constitutionally applied to debts prospectively, but not retroactively.

Chase responded to this situation by retaining the entire text of his opinion that had held the 1862 statute unconstitutional in all instances, then adding a last paragraph which stated that a majority of the Court, were of this view with respect to contracts made before the statute's passage. This left the holding in *Hepburn v. Griswold* unclear. Was the statute completely unconstitutional, or was it unconstitutional retroactively but not prospectively? The newspapers of the day commented on this inconsistency.

Shortly thereafter Justice Grier resigned from the Court. By the time of his resignation, as noted, Congress, with an eye on the legal tender situation, promptly decided to permit the nomination of two additional Justices. William Strong and Joseph Bradley were quickly confirmed. Both would vote to invalidate *Hepburn v. Griswold* in the subsequent *Legal Tender Cases*, which were argued and decided only a year after *Hepburn*.

In the meantime Chase had attempted to prevent any new legal tender cases from coming before the Court, despite the ambiguities in his *Hepburn* opinion. Prior to the new appointments, he pursued this strategy successfully, but as soon as the new Grant appointees were confirmed, they urged clarification of the *Hepburn* opinion. Chase then attempted to use his prerogatives as Chief to keep any new legal tender cases off the docket, and nearly succeeded. Justice Samuel Miller, who had voted against Chase in *Hepburn* and regarded himself as the leader of "pro-greenback" sentiment on the Court, described the Court's internal deliberations to his brother-in-law:

> We have had a desperate struggle in the secret conference of the court for three weeks over two cases involving the legal tender question. The Chief Justice has resorted to all the stratagems of the lowest political trickery to prevent their being heard and the fight has been bitter in the conference room. . . .
>
> The excitement has nearly used me up. It has been fearful; and my own position as leader in marshalling my forces, and keeping up their courage against a domineering Chief, and a party in court who have

> been accustomed to carry everything their own way, has been such a strain on my brain and nervous system as I never wish to encounter again.[7]

Miller was referring to events surrounding a particular conference in March 1870 in which Chase revealed that he had filed an order stating that two cases on the Court's docket which had involved legal tender issues would be "passed" and governed by *Hepburn v. Griswold*. "To my surprise," Chase wrote in his diary, "this statement though supported by Judges Nelson, Clifford & Field, was controverted by Judges Swayne, Miller & Davis; and to my greater surprise," Chase's diary entry continued, "the new Judges [Strong and Bradley] undertook to decide the point against the majority of their brethren."[8] Under pressure, Chase withdrew his order, and the new majority issued an order setting the two cases for argument in early April 1870.

Chase, however, was not yet defeated. He argued that counsel for the litigants in the forthcoming cases had been informed that *Hepburn* would control the results in them, and it was thus unfair to reopen them, especially on such short notice. He even managed to get the lawyers involved to withdraw their appeals, and he then announced that the Court would adjourn at the end of April 1870. He did not succeed, however, in avoiding a rehearing of the constitutionality of the statute invalidated in *Hepburn*, because the new majority simply voted to place on the docket two more legal tender cases which had been working their way up to the Court. These two cases, combined as *The Legal Tender Cases*, were eventually argued in April 1871 and decided in May 1871. Formal opinions in those cases were not to be delivered until January 1872. *The Legal Tender Cases* squarely overruled *Hepburn*, and Chase recorded in his diary that "[i]t is I think a sad day for the country and . . . for the cause of constitutional government. The consequences of the sanction this day given to unredeemable paper currency . . . are sure to come."[9]

In the same diary entry Chase wrote that "[t]he only thing I regret in connection with my administration of the Treasury is that I ever expressed even a qualified opinion that the making the United States notes a legal tender was necessary . . . I regard this as the one blot on my financial system." That passage, taken together with Chase's actions in the sequence of legal tender cases, says much about his conduct as Chief Justice. He was, on the one hand, guided, at least in cases that raised issues on which he held deep convictions, more by principle than by expediency. He not only equated the economic "unsoundness" of making paper money legal tender with the unconstitutionality of that practice, he was "surprise[d]" that any of his fellow Justices would be inclined to revisit the question once he had obtained a majority for his position. This even though his majority was paper-thin and perhaps even nonexistent, even though his own opinion in *Hepburn* had seemingly invited at least a partial reconsideration of its scope, and even though he knew very well that both the incumbent President and a majority of Congress wanted federal greenbacks validated as legal tender.

So one could very well conclude that Chase had hardly acted like an "ambitious politician" in the sequence of legal tender cases. However, Miller had characterized Chase's efforts to avoid reconsideration of the *Hepburn* decision as "stratagems of the lowest political trickery," and they could certainly be seen as such, at least in the context of the Chase Court's internal deliberations. Chase had first, without consulting his fellow Justices, entered an order that suggested *Hepburn* was a far more sweeping decision than it was. Then, when that order was overridden by one inviting continued argument of legal tender issues *Hepburn* had left open, Chase delayed publishing that order, invoked arguments on behalf of litigants who had initially not made them, and attempted to adjourn the Court's Term without any commitment to hear any more legal tender cases. He failed in that effort, as he probably expected to, but he made the effort nonetheless.

Thus, it appears, at least if the *Hepburn* sequence is taken as illustrative, that Salmon P. Chase was not so much a conventional politician in the sense of shaping his opinions with an eye on a prospective constituency for national political office as what might be called a political strategist within the Court's judicial culture. Chase understood the internal powers and prerogatives of the Chief Justiceship and sought to use them to make his office as Chief Justice of the United States more rewarding for him and his colleagues. He also sought to structure the internal deliberative process of the Chase Court to his own advantage. Perhaps this is what Justice Miller meant by his reference to "the selfishness generated by ambition" he found in Chase. But Miller added that in his view Chase was "a great man and a better man than public life generally leaves one."

Endnotes

[1] G. Edward White, "Reconstructing the Constitutional Jurisprudence of Salmon P. Chase," 21 ***No. Ky. L. Rev.*** 41 (1993).

[2] For the quotes from Lincoln and Miller and Davis, *see* David F. Hughes, ***Salmon P. Chase: Chief Justice*** 8 (1963) unpublished Ph.D. dissertation, Princeton University; David F. Hughes, "Salmon P. Chase: Chief Justice," 18 ***Vand. L. Rev.*** 569, 600, 614 (1965). For the quotes from Hayes and Miller, *see* Frederick J. Blue, ***Salmon P. Chase: A Life in Politics*** 320 (1987).

[3] Quoted in David Donald, ed, ***Inside Lincoln's Cabinet*** 261 (1954).

[4] *See* Henry G. Connor, ***John Archibald Campbell*** (1920).

[5] *See* Jacob W. Schucker, ***The Life and Public Services of Salmon Portland Chase*** 240 (1874).

[6] 75 U.S. (8 Wall.) 603, 607 (1870).

[7] Quoted in Charles Fairman, ***Mr. Justice Miller*** 170-171 (1939).

[8] Diary, March 26, 1870, Chase Papers, Historical Society of Pennsylvania, quoted in Charles Fairman, ***Reconstruction and Reunion, 1864-88, Part One*** 740 (1971).

[9] Diary, January 15, 1871, Chase Papers, quoted in *id.*, 759-760.

Justice Embattled:
The Lincoln Administration And The Constitutional Controversy Over Conscription In 1863

Mark E. Neely, Jr.*

The controversy came to a head on Monday morning, September 14, 1863, when President Abraham Lincoln called a special cabinet meeting. Attorney General Edward Bates wrote in his diary afterward that the president was "more angry than I ever saw him." Lincoln reported that Pennsylvania courts were "discharging . . . drafted men rapidly under *habeas corpus*," that the practice was so widespread that it was "defeating the draft," and that he was "determined to put a stop to these factious and mischievous proceedings" if he had the authority. According to Bates, Lincoln said "it was a formed plan of the democratic copperheads, deliberately acted out to defeat the Govt., and aid the enemy. That no honest man did or could believe that the State Judges have any such power." The president threatened to banish the interfering judges to the Confederacy if they persisted in their course. He used the term "bad faith," which was Lincoln's language for describing deliberate partisan malice as opposed to honest difference of opinion on policy. Secretary of War Edwin M. Stanton, Secretary of State William H. Seward, Attorney General Bates, and Secretary of the Navy Gideon Welles essentially agreed with the president, but Secretary of the Treasury Salmon P. Chase and others believed that state judges could discharge persons from the army on writs of *habeas corpus*—underage soldiers, for example—and indeed while serving as a state judge in Missouri before the war, Postmaster General Montgomery Blair had himself done so. Stanton scoffed that federal judges in Pennsylvania were doing it too and indeed that the two worst offenders were John Cadwalader, the U.S. District judge for the Eastern District of Pennsylvania (at Philadelphia) and Wilson McCandless, the judge of the Western District (at Pittsburgh).

That night Lincoln drafted an order for military authorities to answer writs of *habeas corpus* by saying the prisoners were held under the authority of the commander in chief, and if the judge thereafter attempted arrest, the military officer was to resist, "calling to his aid any force that may be necessary to make such resistance effectual." Chase feared that the order would provoke civil war in Pennsylvania and at the follow-up cabinet meeting the next day persuaded Lincoln not to issue it directly but to issue a proclamation suspending the writ of *habeas corpus* in such cases first. That would serve as a sort of public warning and as an appeal to public opinion. In the end Lincoln did that, and crisis was averted. But it was a very close thing and might well have led to serious conflict had it not been for Chase, who could not always be counted on to act as a moderating force within the Lincoln administration.[1]

Thus ended one of the greatest constitutional confrontations of the Civil War North. Though rarely referred to in the history books, it might have caused another civil war, one between Democrats and Republicans, between the judiciary and the executive, between Pennsylvania and the federal government in Washington. It deserves more attention than it has received heretofore, but to understand it fully, some background must be supplied.[2]

The Pennsylvania Election of 1863

The background of the constitutional controversy lay in politics. Because the election calendar in the nineteenth century was markedly different from today's, there was, on average, an important election in the United States every other month of the Civil War, that is, in twenty-four of the forty-eight months of the war's duration. Political considerations could never be far from the president's or any other politician's mind, and they must have been on Lincoln's mind in dealing with Pennsylvania's judges in September 1863, for the state was in the throes of a heated election for governor. Also in contention was one of the five seats on Pennsylvania's Supreme Court, which was a popularly elected body.[3] Moreover, that same September saw the Pennsylvania Supreme Court begin hearings on a case in which the justices would rule conscription unconstitutional. The case, called *Kneedler v. Lane*, was decided in November by three Democratic justices with two Republican justices dissenting.

However, by January it was reversed, because one of the Democratic justices failed to win reelection in the October 1863 state elections, and the Republicans on the court now ruled 3-2 that conscription was constitutional after all.

Recent events made the political season particularly warm. The Army of the Potomac under the leadership of Philadelphia's George Gordon Meade had, only in July, turned back an invasion of Pennsylvania at the Battle of Gettysburg. Ten days after the battle, in nearby New York City, the draft riots occurred. In other states holding elections in 1863 the Democrats had decided on a peace strategy, most notably in Ohio, led by the martyr to civil liberty, Clement L. Vallandigham. The political strategy seems not to have been well suited to a recently invaded state. The Republicans appeared eager enough to attack the Democrats' peace theme in Pennsylvania, arguing that southern military strategy dictated besieging Washington by marching *through* the Keystone state and thus causing the peace advocates to give in to the rebels. One of the Philadelphia Union League's posters for the 1863 campaign proclaimed: "THE ROAD TO PEACE THROUGH PENNSYLVANIA VIA WASHINGTON" and quoted from the Richmond *Enquirer* of September 7, 1863, "Let [General Lee] drive Meade into Washington . . . . He will embolden the Peace party should he again cross the Potomac, for he will show the people of Pennsylvania how little security they have from Lincoln."[4]

The election, to be decided on October 14, pitted incumbent Republican governor Andrew J. Curtin against Democrat George W. Woodward, a justice

The New York City draft riots began on July 13, 1863, ten days after the Battle of Gettysburg. The riots began when a mob stormed a draft headquarters to protest the Conscription Act of 1863. The riots were quelled four days later by Federal troops, but not before more than a thousand people were killed or injured and more than $1,500,000 in damage was done to property.

on the Pennsylvania Supreme Court. The other important contest, for justice of the state Supreme Court, saw Republican Daniel Agnew challenge Walter H. Lowrie, who would write the majority opinion in *Kneedler v. Lane* before leaving the bench and surrendering the majority to the Republicans.

The Pennsylvania Democrats, not as comfortable with the party's peace strategy as in other states, seem to have relied on the race issue, a strategy peculiarly appropriate to the Democratic party's extreme pro-southern leadership in Philadelphia. A group of old patricians with emotional ties to the South had gained control of the party apparatus in the city (people like George Wharton, Charles Ingersoll, Peter McCall, and George W. Biddle). Charles Ingersoll, president of the Central Democratic Club, the Democratic headquarters established in January 8, 1863, had married a Tennessean and was an intemperate critic of the war who had already been arrested once by military authorities and released on a writ of *habeas corpus*. Peter McCall, a Whig turned Democrat, had served as mayor of Philadelphia in the 1840s. Wharton, also a former Whig, served as vice-president of the Central Democratic Club and had been Ingersoll's counsel back in 1862, helping him obtain a writ of *habeas corpus* from federal district judge John Cadwalader. George W. Biddle, another vice president of the club, was a distant cousin of Charles Biddle, who served as state chairman of the Democratic party in 1863 and ran Justice Woodward's gubernatorial campaign, a larger responsibility than usual, because the candidate chose to remain aloof and on the bench.[5]

The southern sympathies of these old Philadelphia aristocrats were so pronounced that they did not realize how far out of step they were with most of the other northern people. They were insensitive and tone-deaf to the vibrations their southern apologies sent out. Wharton, McCall, and Biddle—all Episcopalians, apparently let their names be attached to an invitation written in April 1863 to the Episcopal Bishop of Vermont, John Henry Hopkins, to allow them to republish his Biblical defense of slavery originally composed in the midst of the secession crisis. Bishop Hopkins, a former Pennsylvanian, eagerly obliged. The seven-page pamphlet included belittling denunciations of the "all men are created equal" clause in the Declaration of Independence; in fact, fully a fourth of the work mounted an attack on the Declaration of Independence. The pamphlet was broadly circulated by the Democratic State Central Committee, headed by Charles Biddle, as a campaign document.[6]

The Philadelphia Union League Club, a pioneer in modern methods of spreading a partisan message broadcast, recognized a golden opportunity in this gaffe. They rallied the Bishop of Pennsylvania and a majority of the Episcopal clergy in the state to a denunciation printed that same September 1863 in a poster called "THE VOICE OF THE CLERGY." This surprised Hopkins and likely hurt the Democrats, who counted many Episcopalians among their ranks, including their gubernatorial candidate George W. Woodward. Another Republican poster on the Hopkins pamphlet could with some justification announce the "DEMOCRATIC REPUDIATION OF THE DECLARATION OF INDEPENDENCE."[7]

The Democrats may have been on the defensive on that issue, but summer had brought them an opportunity. Conscription met with massive and violent resistance in New York City in July. The New York City draft riots were the greatest civil disturbance in American history to that date, and the week of rioting that left more than one hundred dead revealed the deep unpopularity of conscription. However, this issue was fraught with danger and difficulty, for while it was true that Americans mostly hated and feared the draft, after July 1863 opposition to the draft was associated with the horrendous riots in New York and denouncing the draft might be equated with anarchism.

The "Lawyers' Conspiracy" against Conscription

Nevertheless, the Republicans were on the defensive on the issue of conscription. None of the posters issued by the Philadelphia Union League referred to the draft. It was a loose ball that only the Democrats could run with. But it would be easy to stumble.

The leadership of the Democratic party in Pennsylvania, and especially the ultraconservative leadership of the party in Philadelphia, was not known for its moderation or politic judgment—hence the Bishop Hopkins pamphlet. In Republican eyes, the Pennsylvania Democrats' attempt to get a court ruling against conscription amounted to a party conspiracy, and at least one historian sympathetic to the Lincoln administration and conscription, John Franklin Leach of the Brookings Institution, has dubbed it part of a "lawyers' conspiracy."[8]

In truth, the conspiracy of lawyers was bipartisan; that is to say, lawyers and politicians in *both parties*, recognizing the raw issue exposed to them by the incredible draft riots of July, schemed to find ways to bring the issue of conscription into the courts. Usually they stated this as a desire to get the issue "settled"—even Lincoln, in a halfhearted way spoke thus to the Democratic governor of New York, Horatio Seymour.[9] But what the lawyers really meant, was to get the issue before *the proper court*, that is, one controlled by their party so that the issue could be decided *their way*.

Thus Massachusetts Republican Governor John A. Andrew and New York law reformer David Dudley Field combined their wits and sent another clever attorney, an army lawyer named Charles F. Blake, to see Lincoln and propose a solution. We do not know exactly what Blake told Lincoln, but we do know the views of Andrew and Field, the men who sent him on his mission to the White House. For his part, Governor Andrew said that he did "not know any tribunal before which . . . [the conscription issues] can be more impartially adjudicated than the Supreme Court of this Commonwealth, which is I believe a Court as little impressible by outside influences as any tribunal in existence." In part Andrew was referring to the fact that the Massachusetts Supreme Court was appointed for life and not elected for terms, as the Pennsylvania and New York justices were. But he probably also meant that they were likely to rule in favor of conscription and the administration. There was only one Democrat on the six-member Massachusetts Supreme Judicial Court. So one-sided were its decisions that the most partisan Republican on the Massachusetts court, Ebenezer Rockwood Hoar, wrote only one dissent in ten years on the bench![10]

The message was clearer in Field's letter, which suggested that a New York strategy would dictate bringing the case "before the Circuit Court of the United States." Field added, "In the meantime I would proceed with the draft of course; as it will be time enough to pause, when the act is declared unconstitutional, an event which I do not think will ever take place."[11]

The Democrats were not the only ones concerned with seeing the conscription issue resolved in court. John A. Andrew (above), the Republican governor of Massachusetts, believed that the Supreme Judicial Court of Massachusetts could impartially decide such cases because the judges were appointed for life, and were not swayed by outside influences.

These Republican strategies did not involve constitutional scruples about whether the ruling should come from a federal court (the New York solution) or a state one (the Massachusetts solution), though members of Lincoln's cabinet had shown much concern and confusion over that issue and there would be much more steam let off over it by opposing judges in later decisions. The essential idea was not that states or the federal government had constitutional control of the matter; the essential idea was that the "settlement" should come from a Republican judge.

The scheme within the Democratic party betrayed similar indifference to constitutional principle and similarly consuming interest in a favorable result. They sought ways to get the issue before courts controlled by Democratic judges, but the Republicans had greatly complicated the Democratic lawyers' problem. In March 1863 Republicans in Congress acted to protect President Lincoln against the consequences of his worst personal failing to date—his tendency to arbitrary executive action and his indifference to constitutional niceties. They passed a law authorizing the suspension of the writ of *habeas corpus*, thus lending to Lincoln's politically vulnerable unilateral action new congressional sanction.[12] The move was as important in Pennsylvania as anywhere. Republican Governor Curtin himself had serious doubts about the constitutionality of suspension of the writ of *habeas corpus* by executive authority and had expressed them publicly.[13] The shrewd move of the Republicans in Congress left the Democrats with one less argument to use against the Lincoln administration, and they were already running short of good arguments.

The Democratic party traditionally campaigned on economic issues, but in 1863 economic conditions were generally favorable to their constituents' interests. Inflation was modest by war-economy standards, and employment opportunities were good, with hundreds of thousands of young laborers in the army and navy. As even a good Democrat like Martin Van Buren's son observed on September 4, 1863, "Thanks to a good farmer, I am promised fair crops and, thanks to the war, they should command fair prices."[14] The national party's 1864 platform would not contain an economic plank.[15]

Prosperity thus left Democrats without their favorite issue, and peace did not seem a viable issue, at least in Pennsylvania, after Gettysburg. The race question was always tempting, but it was difficult to exploit, as the controversy over the Bishop Hopkins pamphlet showed. Furthermore, the suspension of the writ of *habeas corpus* left Democrats without an obvious way of exploiting an explosive new possibility, the draft. It would take more than a simple appeal to justice to secure a constitutional resolution of the issue. The Democrats could not now seek a test before a judge by requesting a writ of *habeas corpus*, for the privilege of the writ had been suspended nationally on September 24, 1862, for any person imprisoned by military authority. Congress' action the next March apparently added only the retroactive sanction of the legislative branch.

The Democratic scheme was not a product of the peculiar extremism of the elite pro-southern Democratic party leadership in Philadelphia. It was, instead, a policy widely agreed upon by Democrats in New York, Pennsylvania, and elsewhere. One of the leaders was Samuel J. Tilden, of New York, a lawyer of considerable reputation and a politician of moderate views.

Tilden initiated a desperate Democratic search for a way to obstruct Republican policies without the use of the writ of *habeas corpus*. He apparently conferred with George Ticknor Curtis, another prominent New York Democratic lawyer, during the week of the draft riots in the city. On July 17, Curtis wrote Tilden, "after much reflection":

> Does not the jurisdiction of our Supreme Court, in General Term, admit of a writ of prohibition, to be applied for on the ground that certain persons, etc., are about to enroll, summon, and subject to martial law A. B. and C. D., citizens of New York and members of its militia, etc., etc.? This would avoid all difficulty about the *habeas corpus*. If it be said that a prohibition out of a State court cannot control a Federal officer, I think it is sufficiently answered if the prohibition is founded on the allegation that the Federal officer is undertaking to act under color of a law constitutionally invalid. The process and the case may be afterwards drawn into the Federal judicial power for revision. But it may issue and may be served, and then there is a Legal process and not a mere forcible resistance.
>
> The Federal court, too, has probably the same jurisdiction, although I have not the means here of looking at that. I should think Judge Nelson could come to town if requested.[16]

Apparently Curtis wanted the New York Supreme Court to issue a writ preventing federal conscription officers from enrolling certain men. About the best that could be said for the idea was that it was better than "mere forcible resistance."

The "Judge Nelson" referred to, of course, was Samuel Nelson of New York, a Justice of the U.S. Supreme Court, a Democrat, and a very improper person to talk to before a case came up testing the constitutionality of conscription. But the United States Supreme Court was not finicky about such

William H. Seward was the elder statesman of the Republican party when President Lincoln appointed him Secretary of State in 1861. In addition to his diplomatic duties, he assisted President Lincoln in discovering the conscription views of Justice Samuel Nelson.

matters. The Chief Justice, Roger B. Taney, had already written an opinion declaring the draft unconstitutional and had it waiting in his desk for the first case that came before him raising the issue![17]

Republicans, with equal impropriety, were also hopeful of Nelson's favor. Secretary of State William H. Seward contrived an elaborate plot to visit Nelson and sound out his views on conscription. Seward's son later described what happened:

> Seward had high confidence in the patriotism, as well as the sound legal judgment of Mr. Justice Nelson . . . . If the questions could come before him they would doubtless be decided rightly, and the factious proceedings would be overruled. But how to get his judgment, or how to confer with him, was a problem. The Judge was at his home in Cooperstown for the summer. The Administration could not call him to Washington, or send to him at Cooperstown, without exciting comment and giving ground for complaint that the Executive was trying to influence the judiciary. And yet, to wait for the questions to reach him by the slow process of law, would waste precious weeks, and be fatal to the reinforcement of the Army, on which every thing depended.
> In this juncture, Seward said he thought he saw a way of rendering the country two services at once. He would invite the leading members of the Diplomatic Corps to make a summer trip, often talked of, with him, through the State of New York. On the way he would stop at Cooperstown and quietly confer with Judge Nelson without attracting attention or exciting comment.

And so it happened that Washington's diplomatic corps toured central New York and spent a night at Cooperstown.[18]

The Democrats had fewer opportunities to influence the judiciary, and their scramble for "settlement" of the conscription question seems more desperate. George T. Curtis' proposed legal remedy, for example, probably would not have worked because it was formed in ignorance of the law. A writ of prohibition is an order from a superior court to an inferior one, meant to protect the jurisdiction of the superior court. It is generally described as a check on judicial power. That it could be applied to appointees of the executive branch to keep them from their duties seems farfetched—let alone by a state court on federal executive appointees. Claudius L. Monell's contemporary *Treatise on the Practice of the Supreme Court of the State of New York* identified the writ of prohibition as a power rarely used, and properly used not against a ministerial officer but against a court. Yet Curtis was one of the greatest lawyers in the land and had served as counsel in the most famous case of the era: *Dred Scott v. Sandford*. Not only was the writ of prohibition idea legally questionable, constitutionally it amounted to exactly what the Republicans would later accuse the Democratic legal measures of being: judicial nullification.[19]

But Curtis' solution, avoiding the obvious jurisdiction he acknowledged in a federal court, had the necessary advantage of bringing the question of conscription before a Democratic court. The Supreme Court of New York was not the highest appellate court in the state, but was rather one of eight district state courts whose judges were elected by the people in district elections. The court for the New York City District was, of course, Democratic in composition, because Democrats had controlled the city for years. One of the sitting judges of the First Judicial District, George G. Barnard, had already addressed the rioting mob in the city and told them in his speech that the conscription law was unconstitutional.[20]

While New York Democrats floundered, Philadelphia feared draft riots too, and the draft began in the fourth congressional district in Philadelphia that same hot July, on the 15th. Democratic lawyers in Pennsylvania began scheming immediately to get conscription before their courts. As early as July 21, 1863, Philadelphian Francis W. Hughes, a moderate who had managed the Democratic campaign in Pennsylvania in the off-year elections the year previous, told Tilden that Pennsylvanians awaited a decision of the New York courts:

> The suspense here to have the adjudication of your courts upon the constitutionality of the conscription act is painful. If the courts shall hold that this enactment is outside of and overrides the Constitution, our people in Penn'a will sustain that position. On the other hand, if the courts shall hold the act constitutional, rather than resist law and invoke anarchy, I do not think there will be any other opposition than sporadic outbreaks and a general fleeing to avoid the compulsory service. I write to ask you that for the sake of the public peace, and I may well add for the sake of republican liberty on this continent, you give your best efforts to obtain a *speedy* decision on this subject.[21]

But these matters are immensely complex, because, as constitutional historians sometimes forget in dwelling on the courts and judges, a case requires some individual litigant, and the Democrats needed to find draftees willing to risk being branded deserters and court-martialed or imprisoned. In Pennsylvania the Democrats were apparently having trouble finding a conscripted soldier willing to take such risks.

On the 28th, Tilden received a letter from William B. Reed, a Pennsylvanian and former Buchanan diplomatic appointee, who in the midst of the secession crisis in 1861 had suggested that Pennsylvania might hold a constitutional convention and cast her lot with the southern confederacy. By 1863 he was openly advocating an armistice and convention of the states, even if it should lead to a permanent severing of the Union. Reed disappointedly reported that

> Our proposed litigation here, as to the conscription law, has thus far failed—from want of courage on the part of the litigant . . . . The form which was adopted by Mr. Ingersoll and Mr. Wharton was that of an injunction bill against the enrolling and drafting officers and the hearing hoped for was before the court *in banc*. I now very much doubt if it will be resorted to. A *habeas corpus* before a single judge on the receipt of notice, which constitutes a technical custody, seems to me preferable.

The extremist Reed found himself "puzzled by the apathy with which it is received, especially in connection with the admitted fact that New York and probably New Jersey are to be exempt. Still, I think there will be an outbreak whenever the actual kidnapping begins."[22] Reed's letter let historians in on the Pennsylvania scheme to get conscription before the Pennsylvania Supreme Court through an injunction bill, that is, in chancery. And he let us know who the schemers were: Philadelphia southern sympathizer Charles Ingersoll and his fellow Philadelphia lawyer and Democrat, George Wharton.[23]

Not all Democrats wanted to see the party challenge the draft. Pennsylvania's most famous Democrat, ex-President James Buchanan, was not as isolated in his country retreat in Wheatland as he appeared to be, and his political instincts were not as bad as they had appeared in the secession crisis two years earlier. On July 25, 1863, he wrote to Augustus Schell about the draft, warning that Governor Seymour in New York was about to "fall into error" by arguing its unconstitutionality. About the same time the ex-President wrote to warn his state's Demo-

James Buchanan returned to his country home, Wheatland, after he left the White House in 1861. He remained interested in politics however, and discouraged his fellow Democrats from pursuing a challenge to the draft.

cratic gubernatorial candidate, George Woodward, not to run on the issue of the draft's unconstitutionality. On September 5, 1863, Buchanan wrote Woodward again, apologizing for having written the previous letter about conscription. He would have refrained had he reflected that Woodward was a justice of the supreme court as well as Democratic candidate for governor. The mixing of party politics and the administration of justice had always been abhorrent to him, Buchanan said. (As President-elect, Buchanan had not been squeamish about asking fellow Pennsylvanian and U.S. Supreme Court Justice Robert Grier how the court was going to rule on the *Dred Scott* case so that he would know what to say in his inaugural address.) Nevertheless he had noticed that the Democratic party in New York was "fast making the unconstitutionality of the Conscription Law the leading and prominent point in the canvass, and I wrote (I believe with good effect) to an able and influential friend, guarding him against it . . . . At the same time it occurred to me that a word of caution to you confidentially, as a candidate, not as a Judge, might not be inappropriate."[24]

The reason for Buchanan's unaccustomed delicacy in the matter was that the scheming Wharton and Ingersoll had by September managed to get up a case to bring conscription before a Pennsylvania state court dominated by Democrats.

The case brought before the Supreme Court of Pennsylvania was most likely a contrived case—a political plot rather than a genuine legal confrontation. It followed precisely the injunction bill strategy described in William Reed's letter two months earlier. It seems improbable that three innocent Pennsylvania draftees decided, when called in September, to hire lawyers and appeal their draft notices. If so, how did they happen to hire four lawyers who included the president and two vice-presidents of the Philadelphia Democratic Club? If so, how did they happen to find the very lawyers clever enough to dream up the injunction scheme discussed among Democrats two months earlier to get around the writ of *habeas corpus* dead end—Charles Ingersoll and George Wharton? If so, why did their team of lawyers also include Peter McCall, another vice-president of the Democratic club and an ex-mayor of Philadelphia, along with George W. Biddle, the cousin of the Democratic state chairman, Charles Biddle?

To obtain an injunction, the plaintiffs had to appeal to chancery court. These lawyers knew that a petition for a writ of *habeas corpus* would bring no relief—only a stonewall response that it had been suspended in such cases. They knew also that the federal route was closed to them, for, although the United States District Judge for the Eastern District of Philadelphia, John Cadwalader, was an old Democrat, he was also an old-fashioned Democrat, cut in the mold of Andrew Jackson, and in a recent case he had upheld the constitutionality of the conscription act. It was a briefly famous decision, called *Antrim's Case*, decided on September 9, 1863, in Philadelphia. And though Cadwalader let the plaintiff, a draftee claiming exemption as the son of a widowed mother dependent on him for support, off on a technicality, he declared, "The general provisions of the act are not unconstitutional."[25]

Given the existence of a deliberate partisan plot to put conscription before the proper judges, was the administration justified in its response to the Pennsylvania constitutional controversy? Should executive prerogative have been defended to the extent of banishing Pennsylvania's judges to the Confederacy and sending troops to resist their decisions? No, it was not justified, because the partisan conspiracy to declare conscription unconstitutional in the Pennsylvania Supreme Court, the plan conceived by Wharton and Ingersoll and McCall and Biddle that eventually became *Kneedler v. Lane*, holding the conscription act unconstitutional—that particular Democratic conspiracy was not the one against which the administration reacted. Lincoln, who instigated the move against the Pennsylvania judges, never mentioned the decision in *Kneedler v. Lane* in any surviving document.

The fact is that *Lincoln reacted to John Cadwalader's decision to let the soldier plaintiff go on a technicality in a decision that otherwise upheld the constitutionality of the conscription act!* Or he reacted, at least in part, to that decision. It should have been quite otherwise. To have a Democratic judge issue such a decision was a godsend, and the Republican dissenters in *Kneedler v. Lane* later approvingly quoted Cadwalader's decision as support for their minority view that conscription was indeed constitutional. Surely there is no better illustration of the indifference to or ignorance of constitutional issues of the key figures in the Lincoln administration, including the president, the secretary of state, the secretary of war, the secretary of the navy, and the attorney general. These politicians had a job to do—win the war—and to do it they needed men in the army. Their principal and proper concern was the impact of judicial decisions on mobilization. If a man eluded the army by means of a judicial decision, the decision should be challenged. They did not read Cadwalader's decision in *Antrim's Case*. Indeed, as Salmon P. Chase discovered to his astonishment when the crisis over Pennsylvania ended, neither the president nor anyone else in the cabinet had even read the conscription statute. They had neither the time nor the inclination to pore over tedious arguments about *nisi prius*, hearings *in banc*, injunction bills, and such. They were men of action first and constitutional lawyers second, if at all.

Judge John Cadwalader of Philadelphia was a Jacksonian Democrat. In an 1863 conscription case, he raised the ire of President Lincoln by allowing a draftee a technical exemption, even though Caldwalder was careful to note that the general provisions of the conscription act were constitutional.

Lincoln and his colleagues were also eager partisans, as were the other actors in this drama, executive officials and judges alike. They failed to notice how small a challenge Cadwalader had offered. In their view, Cadwalader's decision was problematic, first because it let soldiers out of the army, and second, because he was the appointee of James Buchanan, a Democratic president. Their partisan myopia prevented them from seeing that Cadwalader's decision was in fact a Republican's dream come true. Better informed and nearer the scene, Philadelphia diarist Sidney George Fisher, for example, had immediately recognized the potential for Republican exploitation that lay in the Cadwalader decision. Fisher saw in it an important lesson as well:

> *September 19, 1863* There has been a discussion of the President's proclamation suspending the writ of habeas corpus before Jno. Cadwalader, U.S. district judge,

> in which he declared it to be constitutional. He made a similar decision a few weeks ago in relation to the Conscription Act. He is a Democrat. These two opinions, therefore, will have weight with his party & take from the demagogues two of their chief topics of declamation & agitation. The wisdom of the principle of making the judiciary independent is illustrated by the conduct of Cadwalader & Woodward. The former, a U.S. judge, holds his office during good behavior & has, tho an eager partizan, withdrawn from active or ostensible participation in politics and administered his office without party bias, whilst Woodward, a state judge, elected by the people for a term of years, is at this moment a candidate for the place of governor of the state.[26]

In fact, the Republican administration may have been on the verge of banishing Cadwalader to the Confederacy and resisting enforcement of his decision with force of arms, despite the fact that constitutionally *he was on their side*. Partisan pique made them willing to risk civil war in the North.

Kneedler v. Lane

Energetic partisanship tends to magnify the unity and strength of the opposition. American political parties are in fact notoriously diverse and non-ideological, containing voters of many opinions and leaders of several opinions. The differences within Pennsylvania's Democratic party in the middle of the Civil War made for a strange epilogue to the story of the attempt to get up a constitutional test of conscription.

The internal workings of the Pennsylvania state supreme court, like that of any court, are secret. Since the Democrats controlled the court in September, they could probably have brought the case to a decision by election day if they had really wanted to. The Republican majority certainly had little trouble moving quickly the following December in getting the initial decision reversed.

The initial hearing was held on September 23, three weeks before the election on October 13. Instead of acting quickly, however, the court postponed decision until November. Woodward, duly warned by Buchanan, might have had second thoughts and decided it was better merely to call conscription into question than to put himself on record against it before election day. The more moderate wing of the party probably regarded the challenge to the draft as spoiling their chances of capitalizing on constitutional issues; the scheme put the party in the position of criticizing in a partisan manner what was clearly authorized by the Constitution and necessary to win this long war. That, at any rate, had been the upshot of Buchanan's advice. Woodward is said to have responded rather stiffly to Buchanan's letter, but Woodward was a stiff man, and evidently not a fool.[27] The court avoided a showdown with the administration before election day.

In the end, the Republicans fought hard and used all the tricks of the political trade to win the Pennsylvania election in 1863. The country's leading Republican politician, Abraham Lincoln, even issued an election-day dispatch denying that the Army of the Potomac under General Meade had suffered a defeat. Lincoln's dispatch was used in Pittsburgh to parry last-minute rumors circulated by the Democrats that the Union had suffered a serious defeat that very day.[28]

The parties' efforts paid off in results among the electorate. Curtin defeated Woodward, 269,496 to 254,171. Two years earlier, in the presidential election, Lincoln had carried the state with 268,030 votes to 208,412 for his opponents, combined. Thus Curtin gained about 1500 more votes than Lincoln had, and voting rose remarkably, from 476,442 in 1860 to 523,667 in 1863, an increase of 9.9%. Most of the increase came from Democrats, who arrived 46,000 men stronger at the polls than in 1860. Judge Agnew beat Judge Lowrie 267,257 to 254,855.[29]

On November 9, 1863, the Pennsylvania supreme court announced its decision. Justice Lowrie's majority opinion invoked time-honored shibboleths of American republicanism. Recalling "generations of experience of Cavalier and Roundhead, Court and Country, Whig and Tory," he relied on traditional fears that a dominant party would use unconstitutional means to force "the measures which they deemed essential or important for the public welfare, or for securing their own power." And he invoked a brittle states' rights vision, complaining that the draft could destroy the states' militias and leave "the states as defenseless as an ancient city with its walls broken down. Nothing is left that has any constitutional right to stand before the will of the federal government." The walled-in rigidity of his states' rights vision was exceeded only by his fear of party. "There are no constitutional restraints of this power, if it exists, and therefore if the unsteady morality of party excitements will bear it, the party in power may require all the troops to be drafted from the opposite party, or from states and sections where it prevails. Our fathers saw these dangers and intended the constitution to stand as a restraint upon party power."[30]

Justice Woodward's concurring opinion likewise warned of the threat posed by the draft to the militia as the states' ultimate protection from the central government's standing army. He asserted that the framers had particular modes of raising armies in mind when they granted Congress the power, and he also attacked the new conscription law's ability to make a man a deserter before he was mustered in (by declaring it desertion to fail to report to the rendezvous). Like all politically-minded Democrats, he yearned to attack the law's Achilles heel, the thirteenth clause allowing payment of $300 commutation to escape the draft, but admitted that such was "an objection to the spirit of the enactment rather than to its constitutionality." Commutation, unfortunately for the Democrats, was not the issue raised here.[31]

Justice James Thompson's concurring opinion was more legalistic and least resembled a stump speech, though even he could not resist invoking memories of Runneymede at the end. Thompson cited the common law rule that, in the absence of instructions, the customary mode of exercising a legislative power is intended. Such a rule would eliminate direct conscription by the federal government. He argued that the means now used under the conscription statute were so far from customary at the time of the Constitution's origins that it was "preposterous" to imagine that the document would ever have been ratified "if a power had been supposed to exist, to raise an army, not by voluntary means but by coercive." He pointed to *The Federalist* for authority, citing Numbers 24 through 28, especially the last number. The militia, he thought, was "the security of the states against the federal government, and their only security; for the states themselves are not allowed to support armies." Finally, he cited the Bill of Rights with its provision that "a well-regulated militia being necessary to the security of a free state, the rights of the people to keep and bear arms shall not be infringed."[32]

Justice Thompson offered a selective reading of the *Federalist*. Only Number 28 included passages that might sustain his vision. "Power being almost always the rival of power," Hamilton wrote, "the General Government will at all times stand ready to check the usurpations of the state governments; and these will have the same disposition towards the General Government." "It may safely be received as an axiom in our political system," Hamilton added, "that the state governments will in all possible contingencies afford complete security against invasions of the public liberty by the national authority." He did not mention the militia specifically as the states' protection against the federal government's standing army. But Hamilton came closest to saying what *Kneedler v. Lane* argued when he concluded Number 28 with this rhetorical question: "When will the time arrive, that the federal Government can raise and maintain an army capable of erecting a despotism over the great body of the people of an immense empire; who are in a situation, through the medium of their state governments, to take measures for their own defence with all the celerity, regularity and system of independent nations?" The Democratic justices in Pennsylvania wrote about the militia as though it represented the armed force of nearly "independent nations."

On the other hand, nothing in Numbers 24-27 supported the Democrats' position on conscription. Instead, these papers argued that the surest safeguard for liberty was to rest the power to raise armies in the popularly elected Congress. These papers also looked upon the militia as an auxiliary to the standing army in national defense and not as an antagonistic or balancing force representing a different political entity. And what the Democrats neglected to cite from the *Federalist* may have been as significant as what they did. The discussion of the military powers in the *Federalist* actually begins with Number 23, not Number 24, and the first-named included the bald assertion that the power to raise armies and the other powers granted to Congress for the common defense "ought to exist without limitation."[33]

Republican Justices William Strong and John M. Read, in separate dissents, argued that the powers of the federal government were limited in number, not in nature, and were, once enumerated, full and complete. Significantly, Strong left room for future criticism of the commutation fee provision. Read went to *Federalist* Number 23 for authority, and in general his appears to have been the more heavily researched in the precedents.[34]

Justice Lowrie's term expired the first Monday in December, and on the 12th a Republican justice moved to rehear *Kneedler v. Lane*. The court met for the hearing on December 30, and the injunction was reversed on January 16, 1864. The justices did not think it necessary to go over the ground already covered in their opinions of November. Justice Strong offered an extended aside on the use of injunctions and equity in such a case as this one. Read's concurring opinion accused the Democratic justices of nullification, in that they allowed the plaintiffs to avoid the suspension of the writ of *habeas corpus* through an injunction bill. He invoked Taney's opinion in *Ableman v. Booth* as precedent for the position that no state authority could free a federal prisoner by a writ of *habeas corpus* or vice versa—a position more extreme than that taken by several members of Lincoln's cabinet on the question. Finally, the new justice, Daniel Agnew, defended the appropriateness of his decision to reverse what had been so recently decided by the court.[35]

Woodward and Thompson issued a joint dissent complaining that a ruling of the Supreme Court of the United States was needed and was set up by the previous decision. Would the government have moved to rehear the case if Lowrie had been reelected? the Democrats asked pointedly, and they argued that such willingness to rehear cases paved the way to the unsettlement of any decision and lay the court open to hearing and rehearing case after case.[36]

In truth, the Democrats had stopped well short of the greatest provocation, for their original injunction applied only to the three plaintiffs and did not prevent the Fourth District Enrollment Board from continuing its work. For that reason, perhaps, and from the knowledge that the majority of the court was sure to change political complexion soon, the administration took no notice of *Kneedler v. Lane*.

Conclusions

Neglect of this frightening episode in the history of American justice stems from several factors. In the first place, though it was a near miss, it was a miss: in the end nothing really happened. President Lincoln issued another proclamation, but drafting of men and drafting of judicial opinions went on largely unabated. In the second place, it does seem to constitute an anomaly in the workings of the Lincoln administration. Lincoln rarely accused his critics of "bad faith." He was an old partisan himself, and he had high tolerance for partisan conflict. He nearly went over the edge here, perhaps, but this is but a small chapter in a much longer history, the theme of which could arguably be the survival intact of the two-party system, free elections, and an independent judiciary in the midst of a great civil war. Third, the issues are complex and difficult, and it is by no means clear that even the protagonists at the time fully understood them. As Salmon P. Chase observed, even for the cabinet members the provisions of the conscription act "were unfamiliar to all."

And yet, for all its difficulties and anomalous nature, the Pennsylvania constitutional controversy of 1863 cannot be swept under the carpet of inconvenient historical events. Within the often quiet constitutional history of the Civil War, it cries out as an event in need of explanation. So quiet has been the depiction of that history heretofore that it has recently become fashionable to argue that the Constitution shaped the war more than the war shaped the Constitution. Historians have come to describe the constitutional conflicts of the Civil War as "conversations," "dialogue," or "discourse." Clearly the constitutional conflict of 1863 might strain that conclusion, even as it confirms others generally accepted. In the last analysis the episode points up four conclusions that are certainly applicable to Pennsylvania in 1863 and may be true of the Civil War in many areas and at many times.

1. Justice for the most part was not embattled during the Civil War. *Kneedler v. Lane* was the only case in the two thick volumes reporting the Pennsylvania Supreme Court decisions for the January, May, and November terms of 1863 as well as the January term of 1864 that had anything to do with war. The

rest presented ordinary stuff: questions like the conclusiveness of auditors' reports, the effect of the term "acceptance waived," bastardy and fornication, the sale of intoxicating liquors, deciding the next of kin by civil not canon law, removal of fixtures on encumbered real estate, husband and wife, debtor and creditor, divorce, and mechanic's liens. All of this humdrum squabbling over property and family took place in one of the few Union states invaded by a rebel army in the very year it was invaded.

2. War may well have shaped the Constitution more than the Constitution shaped the war. Certainly the members of the administration in Washington, who had a war to fight, showed little interest in constitutional decisions; they did not read them or the statutes they questioned. They looked for ways to get the nation mobilized and to get obstreperous judges out of the way of that goal.

3. The realistic way of phrasing the constitutional questions of the Civil War is to ask how the judges, rather than the Constitution, shaped the war or were shaped by it. Such an approach allows us to understand their actions, for their actions make little sense without the mediating institution of political parties. *Kneedler v. Lane* could have no other meaning, with its quick and nakedly partisan reversal of opinion after the Pennsylvania state election of 1863.

4. The Democrats in their zeal to fight the Republicans indulged in judicial nullification of the laws of Congress. For their part, the Republicans proved willing to risk civil war within Pennsylvania. Parties could strain, if not quite break, the bonds of Union. And justice could not always restrain them.

Endnotes

* I want to thank Trey Wilson, a student at St. Louis University School of Law, and Sylvia Neely for help with the research; Phillip Shaw Paludan read and criticized the manuscript before publication; our continuing "conversation" on the Constitution during the Civil War has been useful to me, as well as enjoyable. Professor Iver Bernstein, of Washington University in St. Louis, gave the manuscript a searching reading and offered suggestions from which I greatly benefited.

1 John Niven, ed., ***The Salmon P. Chase Papers, Volume I Journals, 1829-1872*** (Kent, Ohio: Kent State University Press, 1993), pp. 441-444; Howard K. Beale, ed., ***The Diary of Edward Bates, 1859-1866*** (Washington: GPO, 1933), 306-307.

2 The *Merryman* decision of Roger B. Taney in 1861 was also a crisis averted, in that instance because Lincoln ignored the decision and Taney felt it hopeless to enforce. The Pennsylvania crisis and the related Pennsylvania Supreme Court case receive fullest treatment from a constitutional historian in Harold Hyman's ***A More Perfect Union: The Impact of the Civil War and Reconstruction on the Constitution*** (New York: Alfred A. Knopf, 1973), 221-223. Hyman attempts to exempt Lincoln from blame, saying: "Washington prepared for confrontations involving the national Army against federal and state courts, which could only benefit the Confederacy. Simultaneously, Lincoln and congressional leaders tried to work out better ways to sustain the nation without an 'open rupture,' ([William] Whiting's phrase) with any judges." (page 222) I have argued elsewhere that President Lincoln, probably with Stanton's help, instigated the crisis; see ***The Fate of Liberty: Abraham Lincoln and Civil Liberties*** (New York: Oxford University Press, 1991), 69-73. The literature on *Kneedler v. Lane* is not yet equal to the significance of the case. In addition to Hyman's treatment see: J.L. Bernstein, "Conscription and the Constitution: The Amazing Case of *Kneedler v. Lane*, "***American Bar Association Journal***, LIII (1967), 708-712; J.W. Delahant, "A Judicial Revisitation Finds *Kneedler v. Lane* not so 'Amazing,'" ***American Bar Association Journal***, LIII (1967), 1132-1135; and, by far the most valuable treatment, John Franklin Leach, ***Conscription in the United States: Historical Background*** (Rutland, Vermont: Charles E. Tuttle, 1952), 374-383.

3 Roy F. Nichols, ***The Disruption of American Democracy*** (orig. pub. 1948; New York: Free Press, 1967), 20-21; Mark E. Neely, Jr., "The Civil War and the Two-Party System," in James M. McPherson, ed., ***We Cannot Escape History*** (Champaign: University of Illinois Press, 1995). On the Pennsylvania election see Erwin Stanley Bradley, ***The Triumph of Militant Republicanism: A Study of Pennsylvania and Presidential Politics, 1860-1872*** (Philadelphia: University of Pennsylvania Press, 1964), 169-178 and Arnold Shankman, "For the Union as It Was and Constitution as It Is: A Copperhead Views the Civil War," in James I. Robertson, Jr., and Richard M. McMurry, eds., ***Rank and File: Civil War Essays in Honor of Bell Irvin Wiley*** (San Rafael, California: Presidio Press, 1976), 100-106.

4 "A Collection of the Posters and Broadsides Issued by

the Union League of Philadelphia, 1862-1865," The Huntington, San Marino, California. Perhaps collected by Francis Lieber, whose papers are also at the Huntington, the collection consists of large broadsides, folded and bound into a specially made volume.

[5] William Dusinberre, ***Civil War Issues in Philadelphia, 1856-1865*** (Philadelphia: University of Pennsylvania Press, 1965), p. 171, 31; Nicholas B. Wainwright, "The Loyal Opposition in Civil War Philadelphia," ***Pennsylvania Magazine of History and Biography***, LXXXVIII (July 1964), 298-299; Irwin F. Greenberg, "Charles Ingersoll: The Aristocrat as Copperhead," ***Pennsylvania Magazine of History and Biography***, XCIII (April 1969), 190-217; According to Greenberg (page 194), the Democratic party split in 1860, and the Breckinridge faction was led by an elite while the Douglas faction was led by working class and immigrant champion Lewis Cassidy.

[6] John Henry Hopkins, ***A Scriptural, Ecclesiastical, and Historical View of Slavery, . . . Addressed to the Right Rev. Alonzo Potter . . . .*** (New York: W.I. Pooley & Co., 1864), esp. 45, 24.

[7] "Collection of the Posters and Broadsides Issued by the Union League of Philadelphia"; see also Hopkins, ***Scriptural, Ecclesiastical, and Historical View of Slavery***, 42-44.

[8] Leach, ***Conscription in the United States***, p. 362.

[9] Roy P. Basler et al., eds., ***Collected Works of Abraham Lincoln***, 9 vols. (New Brunswick, New Jersey: Rutgers University Press, 1953-1955), VI, 370.

[10] John A. Andrew to Edwin M. Stanton, 22 July 1863, Abraham Lincoln Papers, Library of Congress (microfilm). Moorfield Storey and Edward W. Emerson, ***Ebenezer Rockwood Hoar: A Memoir*** (Boston: Houghton Mifflin, 1911), p. 120. Partisan identifications of the Massachusetts Supreme Court justices were pieced together from the following sources: Leonard W. Levy, ***The Law of the Commonwealth and Chief Justice Shaw: The Evolution of American Law, 1830-1860*** (orig. pub. 1957; New York: Harper & Row, 1967), esp., 337-339; John R. Mulkern, ***The Know-Nothing Party in Massachusetts: The Rise and Fall of a People's Movement*** (Boston: Northeastern University Press, 1990), 71; William T. Davis, ***History of the Judiciary of Massachusetts*** (orig. pub. 1900; New York: DaCapo, 1974); William T. Davis, ***Bench and Bar of the Commonwealth of Massachusetts***, 2 vols. (orig. pub. 1895; New York: DaCapo, 1974).

[11] David Dudley Field to Abraham Lincoln, 19 July 1863, Abraham Lincoln Papers.

[12] See George Clarke Sellery, ***Lincoln's Suspension of Habeas Corpus as Viewed by Congress***, Bulletin of the University of Wisconsin No. 149 (Madison: April, 1907). He describes the debate largely as a contest between congressional and presidential authority; surely there was also at work a common Republican desire not to allow the Democrats to beat them with the issue in future elections.

[13] Neely, ***Fate of Liberty***, 73-74. Curtin's message about *habeas corpus* appeared in February and likely had some hastening effect on Congress in pushing through the *Habeas Corpus* Act of March 3, 1863.

[14] John Bigelow, ed., ***Letters and Literary Memorials of Samuel J. Tilden***, 2 vols. (orig. pub. 1908; Port Washington, New York: Kennikat Press, 1971), I, 184.

[15] Arthur M. Schlesinger, Jr., and Fred L. Israel, eds., ***History of American Presidential Elections, 1789-1968***, 4 vols. (New York: Chelsea House, 1971), III, 1179-1180.

[16] Bigelow, ed., ***Letters and Literary Memorials of Samuel J. Tilden***, I, 175.

[17] John O'Sullivan and Alan M. Meckler, eds., ***The Draft and Its Enemies: A Documentary History*** (Urbana: University of Illinois Press, 1974), 80-92.

[18] Frederick Seward, ***Seward at Washington, as Senator and Secretary of State. A Memoir of His Life, with Selections from His Letters, 1861-1872*** (New York: Derby and Miller, 1891), p. 185; Leach, ***Conscription in the United States***, 355-356.

[19] ***Words and Phrases***, XXXIV, 465-466; Claudius Monell, ***A Treatise on the Practice of the Supreme Court of New York***, 2 vols. (2nd ed.; Albany: Gould, Banks & Co., 1853), I, 261.

[20] On New York's judiciary see Alden Chester, ed., ***Legal and Judicial History of New York***, vol. I (Buffalo, New York: William S. Hein, 1983), 379-380, and Iver Bernstein, ***The New York City Draft Riots: Their Significance for American Society and Politics in the Age of the Civil War***, (New York: Oxford University Press, 1990), 47. For party identification of judges in New York's First Judicial District see ***New York Times***, November 4, 1857, 1; November 7, 1859, 5; Judge Clerke had been endorsed by both parties when he ran in 1861.

[21] Bigelow, ed., ***Letters and Literary Memorials of Samuel J. Tilden***, I, 176; on Hughes see Arnold Shankman, ***The Pennsylvania Antiwar Movement, 1861-1865*** (Rutherford, New Jersey: Fairleigh Dickinson University Press, 1980), 97-98.

[22] Bigelow, ed., ***Letters and Literary Memorials of Samuel J. Tilden***, I, 179. On Reed see Dusinberre, 108 and 157-158.

[23] On injunctions and chancery see Lawrence M. Friedman, ***A History of American Law*** (New York: Simon and Schuster, 1973), 23-24, 130-131, 347.

[24] John Bassett Moore, ed., ***Works of James Buchanan***, 12 vols. (Philadelphia: J.B. Lippincott, 1908) Vol. XI 346; Leach, ***Conscription in the United States***, 361-362.

[25] 1 F. Cas. 1062, at 1054 (D.C.E.D. Pa.) (Case No. 495).

[26] Nicholas Wainwright, ed., ***A Philadelphia Perspective: The Diary of Sidney George Fisher Covering the Years 1834 -1871*** (Philadelphia: Historical Society of Pennsylvania, 1967), 461.

[27] Arnold M. Shankman, ***The Pennsylvania Antiwar Movement, 1861-1865***, p. 133.

[28] ***Collected Works of Lincoln***, VI, 512; Wayne McVeagh to Abraham Lincoln, October 13, 1863; James K. Moorehead to Abraham Lincoln, October 15, 1863, Abraham Lincoln Papers.

[29] ***Tribune Almanac and Political Register for 1864*** (New York: The Tribune Association, 1864), p. 58.

[30] 45 Pa. State 243, 246.

[31] *Id.*, at 254, 260, 253.

[32] *Id.*, at 266, 267, 269, 268, 271-272.

[33] Jacob E. Cooke, ed., ***The Federalist*** (Middletown, Connecticut: Wesleyan University Press, 1961), pp. 179-180, 153, 170, 147.

[34] 45 Pa. State 277, 283, 290.

[35] *Id.*, at 295, 301, 307.

[36] *Id.*, at 329.

The Undocketed Constitutional Bridge Across The War Gulf, ca. 1861-73

Harold M. Hyman

I begin with T. S. Eliot's admonition:

We shall not cease from exploration
And the end of all our exploring
Will be to arrive where we started
And know the place for the first time.

And with lines from W. H. Auden:

Law, says the judge as he looks down his nose,
Speaking clearly and most severely, Law is as I've told you before, Law is as you know I suppose, Law is but let me explain it once more, Law is, the Law.
Yet law-abiding scholars write . . . Law is our Fate; Others say . . . Law is no more Law has gone away.

In late 1862, veteran political activist Elizur Wright asked rhetorically: "Do we condemn the great constitutional bridge which has carried the nation safe . . . from beggary to the front rank of the civilized nations? On the contrary, the less we count ourselves its bond-servants, the more we venerate it. It is a most excellent bridge . . . and if it ever comes to harm it will be from those who seem determined that no part of any flood shall reach the sea except by going under its arches."[1]

In 1945, when many Americans still believed that the Constitution was a machine that would go of itself, they celebrated total victory in what, unforeseeably, was to be their nation's last declared war. Since then, Korea, Vietnam, Bay of Pigs, Desert Storm, Iran-Contra, Somalia and other once-exotic place names and labels head a longish list of undeclared, presidentially initiated, overt and covert armed interventions abroad. After a decade-long effort to diminish recurring political and constitutional crises, Congress created the 1973 War Powers Act. But after its passage as before, each *de facto* war generated divisive domestic controversies about judicial and/or legislative checks on the Commander-in-Chief's war-making initiatives and domestic emergency powers.[2] And as Oliver North's career suggests, in the 1990s final answers are far from in.

In 1861 no think tanks, specialist scholars, or ready bibliographies illuminated analogous concerns. Like the Supreme Court's docket, with rare exceptions legal education and practice seemed then to be irrelevant to the crisis. Declared wars in 1812 and 1846 and numerous short-of-war naval landing parties on distant shores offered little guidance to officials on how to conduct a civil war. Historical memories of domestic disturbances were of Presidents' martial initiatives against whiskey rebels, Indian tribesmen, Kansas pro- and antislavery militants, and fugitive slaves' would-be rescuers. (To anticipate, because of the Civil War's unanticipatable military and political decisions and constitutional readjustments, in the 125 years since Appomattox federal armed force would inhibit, among others, Ku Kluxers, Pullman strikers, liquor bootleggers, and active opponents of "Second Reconstruction" school integrationists and freedom marchers, and Branch Davidians.)[3]

This unpreparedness to deal with the Civil War

was common South and North. Unlike those northward, however, Confederate legalists shared in southern whites' consensus that secession had settled the region's constitutional arrangements as perpetually as slavery froze race relationships. Relatively few southern law writers felt impelled to reexamine war issues. Basic wartime concerns were to be unjusticiable in practical terms. No Supreme Court came into existence, though allowed for in the Confederacy's Constitution. And the absence of two-party adversary politics in Dixie deprived complainants of essential vehicles for advancing constitutional grievances.[4]

In contrast to the South's relatively static legal scene, from Sumter on northern law writers and practitioners impelled themselves into legal research that supported or opposed war policies. Important legal activists and theorists including Salmon P. Chase, Francis Lieber, and William Whiting, all of whom Lincoln brought into his administration, filled in information gaps. In 1861 they enlisted history on the Union's side in "adequacy of the Constitution" analyses so effectively that a contemporary reviewer of their writings marveled because the ". . .apparatus for studying our Constitution has improved more rapidly since the integrity of the Union was threatened than at any preceding period."[5]

Forward-looking rather than static, the "adequacy" consensus was that if kept accountable to constitutionally prescribed civilian overlords in both the White House and Congress, the Union's amassing military power could enhance, not degrade individual liberties, state-centered federalism, and economic capitalism. An astute lawyer-politician, Lincoln was predisposed toward adequacy arguments from his prewar antislavery-extension experience in Illinois Republican party politics, especially after the 1857 *Dred Scott* decision and his losing campaign in 1858 for the U.S. Senate. An educable constitutionalist, Lincoln, in company with like-thinking Senators and Representatives, by 1862 fully endorsed elastic adequacy assumptions. They were, he stressed, implicit in the Constitution's Art. 2, sec. 3 requirement that Presidents "take care" faithfully to execute the laws. Therefore he advised the nation both that "The dogmas of the *quiet* past are inadequate to the stormy present," *and* that the Constitution's war powers were "our main reliance."[6]

Lincoln's insights were plausible because Union soldiers bought time during which adequacy researchers dredged up reliable instances of earlier Presidents who, with or without legislative authority, assigned armed forces to protect missionaries and merchants, suppress seaborne slave traders, crush slave revolts, and recapture runaway slaves. Adequacy writers' analyses popularized also Supreme Court Justice Joseph Story's 1827 opinion rejecting War of 1812 state militiamen's objections to being federalized by President Madison. Story had stated: "We are all of opinion, that the authority to decide whether the exigency has arisen, belongs exclusively to the President, and that his decision is conclusive upon all other persons."[7]

Antiwar legal spokesmen, however, possessed significant advantages. Lincoln's initiatives, especially the anti-disloyalty arrests of civilians by soldiers, were "an astonishment and a puzzle to the people," remembered influential constitutional commentator John C. Hurd. They were also a godsend to antiwar, racist, "Union as it was" conservatives. The latter exhumed one-term Congressman Lincoln's failed "spot resolution" a dozen years earlier that questioned where American soldiers incurred casualties in border skirmishes that justified the formal declaration of War against Mexico. When protesting President Lincoln's "arbitrary arrests" and other Civil War internal security policies, critics, anxious to disassociate themselves and the Democratic party from secession taints, resurrected the Bill of Rights as defense of whites'-only rights against federal deprivations. Antiwar activists gained a potent spokesman in the person of Chief Justice of the United States Roger B. Taney, who, from *Ex parte Merryman* in 1861 until his death in late 1864, misrepresented Magna Carta and the habeas writ as effective bulwarks of whites' liberties since the dawn of America's history.[8]

Then and since, the Lincoln-Taney constitutional clash polarized major constitutional and legal estimates into hero-villain, "showdown" terms. Yet the Lincoln versus Taney approach retains merit as a research tool,[9] merit that Sophocles sketched in Antigone: "You cannot learn of any man the soul, the mind, and the intent, until he shows his practice of . . . government and law. For . . . who controls the state and does not hold to the best plans of all, but

Chief Justice Roger B. Taney clashed with President Lincoln on constitutional matters during the Civil War. In *Merryman*, Taney ruled that Congress alone had the power to declare war, an action Congress would not risk politically.

locks his tongue up through some kind of fear . . . he is the worst of all who were and are."[10]

The first Taney-Lincoln confrontation occurred in the very wake of Fort Sumter's surrender. "King Linkum I," as critics quickly derided him, authorized soldiers to arrest civilian security risks. Nominally on circuit, in *Merryman* Taney reserved to Congress alone a duty it would not accept, of formally declaring war in an undeclarable civil war. As a recent compelling estimate concluded, Taney shaped the *Merryman* clash in order to make an argument "so persuasive that the full Court would agree with him and thus pit the power of the federal judiciary against Lincoln."[11] And recent scholarship concludes also that Taney resorted to legal and historical fictions in order to inhibit not merely the administration's early anti-disloyalty improvisations but its capacity to carry on the war at all.

So aiming, in *Merryman* Taney bypassed adequacy analysts' disagreeable historical evidence about the American Revolution considered as a civil war and about White House initiations of earlier *de facto* conflicts. He resorted instead to ahistorical arguments from Magna Carta, Locke, *habeas* history, and the intentions of *some* Framers (avoiding Hamilton's *Federalist* No. 23, however). These sources were already familiar to contemporaries from the decades-long debates on slavery-related issues, and in *Merryman* Taney ballooned them into precious keys to all Americans' liberties against excessive authority, which they had never been.

Taney's historical hyperbole were vulnerable to important rejoinders by respected contemporary legalists. As example, Horace Binney wrote that:[12]

> . . . the power of Congress over this *[habeas corpus suspension]* matter has never been decided, authoritatively; and it has never been argued . . . in Court [Binney wrote]. So far as authority goes, it is at this time, a question of the first impression. . . . Chief Justice Taney's opinion in Merryman's case is not an authority. . . . He does not argue the question from the language . . . or . . . the history of the [habeas corpus] clause . . . except by an elaborate depreciation of the President's office, even . . . making him, as Commander-in-Chief of the Army . . . no more than an assistant to the [federal] Marshal's posse: the deepest plunge of judicial rhetoric.

Privately, Justice John Catron derided Lincoln's defense of Merryman's arrest as befitting "the reign of Tibereas; its limits should be looked for in Tacitus."[13] But three years would pass before Taney's *Merryman* views gained a place on the Court's docket. When they did, although several Justices sympathized with Taney's static constitutional views, they were less willing than he to compound *Dred Scott* mistakes by again condemning actions by the nation's coordinate governing branches. Since 1787 the Court had done so only twice, in *Marbury v. Madison* and *Dred Scott*, the last with awful consequences nationally. And so in the 1864 *Vallandigham* hearing, the Justices, by then reinforced with Lincoln appointees, would deny themselves jurisdiction of a civilian's appeal from the judgment of a military Court.[14]

Which suggests why, in terms of formally adjudicated war issues, the Court's docket seems at first glance to be a shallow research pool. Politics and battles more than litigations decided public policies.

Thomas Wilson Dorr was the reform governor of Rhode Island during the Dorr Rebellion over the state's antiquated constitution that denied suffrage to most of the urban population. He was convicted of treason by the state judges aligned with the incumbent government. In *Luther v. Borden*, a case stemming from the rebellion, Chief Justice Taney skirted the difficult political issues by invoking the political questions doctrine. This doctrine diverts responsibility for resolving certain constitutional questions to the executive and legislative branches.

But jurists' views were heavy guns in the external political clashes.

Taney never changed his conclusions of 1861—that the nation's military institutions and almost all national institutions except the judiciary, were so inherently uncontrollable by civilian authorities as to doom constitutional government, individuals' liberties, all property rights, federalism, and legal procedure. His perception that only a static society safeguarded rights was reiterated in judges' charges to juries, politicos' stump speeches, ministers' sermons, and editorials. It informed standpat and reactionary constitutional, political, and race relations positions throughout the War and Reconstruction, and anti-race equality activists revived it during our Second Reconstruction.

To counter Taney's large influence, Binney, Lieber, Whiting, and other pro-administration legal writers repetitively used his own 1849 *Luther v. Borden* "political question" doctrine against him. The *Luther* case arose from Rhode Island's mini-civil war known as the Dorr Rebellion. Deciding *Luther*, Taney insisted that authority had to exist somewhere in the national government to decide which of two claimants was legitimately a state. He concluded that Congress not the Court was the proper branch.

Then in the 1857 *Dred Scott* decision Taney discounted his own *Luther* "political question" doctrine, denied to any national branch a power to bar slaves, a state-defined private property, from the national territories, and transformed the Fifth Amendment of the Bill of Rights into a defense primarily of slave owners' property rights. Further contradicting his eagerness to have the whole Court accept jurisdiction of *Merryman* and *Vallandigham*-like issues, in 1858 Taney had joined in a unanimous Supreme Court decision denying itself jurisdiction of a sailor's appeal from a Navy court's penal judgment.[15]

In 1861 fear as well as partisanship inspired the Lincoln Republicans' eagerness to diminish Taney's stature as a guide to individuals' rights against government's wrongs. For, among other hangover prewar issues, a petition was then before the Supreme Court to docket *Lemmon v. New York.*

Inspired in its latter phases by potentialities in *Dred Scott*, the *Lemmon* case was intimately related to the Civil War's causes, and could, if decided in the Supreme Court on *Dred Scott* bases, govern the war's conduct and goals. In 1852 the Lemmons, Virginians, with eight slaves had planned to board ship in New York City for Texas but local antislavery activists sued to halt their exit. Then in 1860 the state's highest court affirmed that New York laws barred slavery and freed the Lemmon's slaves. Meanwhile in *Dred Scott*, Justice Nelson, who supported Taney's major positions, had provided the Lemmon's lawyer with a ground for an appeal:[16]

> Although . . . not before us [Nelson stated] . . . a question has been alluded to . . .

> namely: the right of a master with his slave[,] of transit into or through a free State, on business or commercial pursuits, or in the exercise of a Federal right, or the discharge of a Federal duty, being a citizen of the United States. . . . This question . . . turns upon the rights and privileges secured to a common citizen . . . under the Constitution of the United States. When that question arises, we [Justices] shall be prepared to decide it.

In the heated context of the first wartime spring, fears and hopes were reasonable that the Supreme Court, its roster substantially unchanged since *Dred Scott*, would docket both *Merryman* and *Lemmon*. Then Nelson's *Dred Scott* opinion and Taney's *Merryman* positions might prevail. Foreseeable consequences included unpreventable and unpunishable disloyal acts and permanent disunion. Or, as in the political "compromises" of 1820, 1850, and 1854, perhaps another sectional sellout to the white South might re-wed the seceded states to the Union, but only on their ever-escalating terms.

In the 1860-61 winter the South's leaders had rejected as inadequate a Thirteenth Amendment proposal to the Constitution, unamendably guaranteeing national protection for slave owners' state-defined property rights. Might reunification minima of 1861 transcend even this nightmarish escalation plus other potentialities from *Dred Scott*, *Lemmon*, and *Merryman*? If so, then despite free states' constitutions and the Northwest Ordinance, slavery would be nationalized by Supreme Court decisions plus the unamendable pro-slavery Thirteenth constitutional amendment proposal and the nation's military power would be used primarily against fugitive slaves and their abettors.[17]

The Lemmons' lawyer let their appeal die and, as noted, *Merryman* case issues remained undocketed for three years. In effect Merryman plea-bargained, swore loyalty to the Union, and sat out the war. Again as suggested, Taney kept trying further to shape the whole Court's docket. Scholars long misapprehended that threatened retaliations on the federal judiciary by exacerbated Republicans frustrated Taney's docketing design. Instead, we know now that a Chief Justice's power to set the Court's docket was limited. Taney's successor as Chief Justice, Salmon Portland Chase, deflated correspondents' "vastly misconceived" notions about a Chief's authority. Merely first among equals, it was only on circuit ". . . that the Chief Justice, or any other Judge of the Supreme Court, has, individually, any considerable power."[18]

Therefore some wartime Justices decided matters individually that, otherwise, might have won docket space. For example, in 1861, in chambers, Justice Wayne retroactively ratified Lincoln's unilateral extension of ninety-day militia service to three years.[19] In several instances Justices were reluctant to docket certain matters in deference to statutes or customs. For example, in 1861 an appeal was before the Court from George Gordon, the president of Iberia College in Ohio. The year before he had forcefully blocked the return of a fugitive slave to his master. Convicted of violating the 1850 Fugitive Slave Law, Gordon appealed to the Supreme Court which, as per statute, denied itself jurisdiction in criminal appeals. In early 1862 Lincoln pardoned Gordon.

Almost simultaneously, the Court heard an appeal to review the death sentence of another Gordon, the notorious Nathaniel, a maritime slaverunner. For the Court, Taney rejected Nathaniel Gordon's appeal on the same statutory grounds that had governed its denial to George Gordon, and in this instance Lincoln refused a pardon.[20]

Two momentous years later, in 1863, issues basic to the war's causes, conduct, and purposes did gain a place on the Court's docket. The Justice's frighteningly thin 5-4 *Prize Cases* decision sustained the validity of Lincoln's early blockade orders, and when *Roosevelt v. Meyer* appellants alleged the unconstitutionality of wartime paper money as legal tender, the Court avoided a need adversely to decide. Then, as noted, in 1864 the Justices rejected jurisdiction of Vallandigham's appeal from an adverse judgment of a Union Army military court for aiding the Confederacy through his utterances.[21]

Viewed from these superficially non-war facets, the Court's docket illuminates the cause of the Justices' most pressing fears. Their top-of-agenda apprehensions were not about retribution from the White House and Capitol Hill, about the southern states' wrongs done to generations of black residents, or even about the conduct of the Civil War. Instead, if the Court's wartime docket is a guide, the high jurists were most passionately concerned with northern cities' fiscal and political immoralities.

In 1863, the year of the *Prize Cases* decision, Gettysburg, Vicksburg, and Lincoln's implementation of his Emancipation Proclamation, the *Gelpcke v. Dubuque* decision, wrote the Supreme Court Reporter, enforced "high moral duties . . . upon a whole [northern urban] community, [which was] seeking apparently to violate them."[22]

The *Gelpcke* case arose because Dubuque, with voters' approval, attracted railroad facilities by issuing municipal bonds far in excess of debt limits in Iowa's constitution. Debt repudiations and litigations evoked contrary legislative actions and state supreme court judgments on, among other matters, definitions of Iowa's constitution. In *Gelpcke*, the Supreme Court of the United States disregarded its own tradition that the most recent judgment of a state's highest court on its state constitution should rule in the federal courts. Instead the Court made itself the final judge of which conflicting judgments to honor of successive Iowa popular referenda and conflicting decisions by popularly-elected state supreme court jurists on Iowa's constitution, and fiscally bound Dubuque and cities generally when exercising delegated state powers.

Enormous urban growth would occur after Appomattox. *Gelpcke*-like controversies about cities' debt limits would mark the Granger-to-New Deal half-century. In 1885 a legal writer asserted that the issue of cities' fiscal initiatives authorized by delegations of parent states' powers "has not passed into written history." What did enter history from *Gelpcke* was the federal judiciary's eagerness to stabilize economic interests even at the cost of frustrating cities' efforts to create adequate urban infrastructures, by itself monitoring what another commentator of the 1880s called "the borderland of federal and state court decisions."[23]

Although aggressive concerning its jurisdiction over state matters as in *Gelpcke*, Taney's fellow-jurists were less ready than he to compound *Dred Scott* excesses by again condemning actions by either of the nation's coordinate branches. The Justices took belated cognizance of the fact that since 1789 the Court had done so only twice, in *Marbury v. Madison* and *Dred Scott*. In addition to the extended time lags then common in judicial proceedings, this unspoken commitment by the majority of Justices suggests a reason why the Supreme Court's wartime docket resembles those of pacific prewar decades in accommodating primarily commercial law interests.

Though denied his larger purposes, Taney exploited opportunities on circuit to advance antiwar constitutionalism to fellow professionals and, through them, to the larger public. For example, in mid-1863, on circuit, he again castigated Lincoln, this time for a federal sting operation that "seduced and betrayed" evaders of trade restrictions.[24] But only minorities among fellow-jurists, law practitioners, and, ultimately, voters, sustained him.

Expressing themselves in America's unique wartime elections, balloting majorities, including even soldier-voters, sustained instead Lincoln's orders emancipating slaves, recruiting blacks into Union armed forces, and reconstructing seceded states. And the Congress, its ranks rich in lawyers, sanctioned every executive expedient with statutes, budgets, or both.[25]

When Lincoln told them of his decision to emancipate, the Cabinet officers sat stunned, "still thinking," one remembered vividly, "of what they had just heard, and the future it opens." Confirming this sense of beginnings, Lincoln noted to the nation that "[t]he policy of emancipation, and of employing black soldiers, gave to the future a new aspect, about which hope, and fear, and doubt contended in uncertain conflict." If implemented by the Army, sanctioned by voters, and not disallowed in Congress or the Court, he continued, his war power orders on emancipation and reconstruction would drastically and beneficently enlarge the war's results as measured by its causes.[26]

Congress' exercises of war powers also looked to an improved future. Escalating like Lincoln's executive orders, laws multiplied on conscription, loyalty tests for federal officeholders, an income tax, and legal tender. Statutes successively confiscated convicted traitors' property including slaves, forbade the return of fugitive slaves, repealed the fugitive slave law, and abolished slavery in the District of Columbia and federal territories among other rebuttals to the *Dred Scott* majority. Responding to Lincoln's concern about the Justices reversing emancipation, in early 1865, Congress, with his enthusiastic ap-

When President Lincoln first read the Emancipation Proclamation to his Cabinet members they were reportedly stunned into silence. Seated: (from left) Edwin McMasters Stanton, Abraham Lincoln, Gideon Welles, William Henry Seward and Edward Bates. Standing: (from left) Salmon Portland Chase, Caleb Blood Smith and Montgomery Blair.

proval, as noted earlier sent to the states the present Thirteenth Amendment. The depth of the "war gulf" is the distance between the war's causes, declared aims, and results; between the aborted Thirteenth Amendment proposal of 1860-61 perpetuating slavery and the Thirteenth Amendment of 1865, abolishing it.

Even early considerations of "freedom national," as antislavery lawyers labelled the long-unrealizable aspiration, involved legal as well as constitutional problems. To repeat, a slave was a state-defined private property and the sacredness of property rights was real not a fiction in prewar America. Lincoln limited his military emancipation proclamation geographically to states then still rebelling. But, educable, he was attracted by ideas expressed by the impressive phalanx of proudly self-described Radical Republicans who mixed wartime adequacy constitutionalism with prewar "freedom national" ideas.

Which even in 1862 allowed conservative Democrats to raise disquieting questions about blacks' legal, constitutional, political, and social place in a post-victory America. Responsively, in mid-1862 Lincoln asked Attorney General Edward Bates to define Americans' civil rights deriving from the nation since 1789. A more realistic legal historian than Taney, Bates replied that "Eighty years of practical enjoyment of [national] citizenship, under the Constitution, have not sufficed to teach us either the exact meaning of the word, or the constituent elements of the thing we prize so highly."[27]

True. But by mid-1863 Congress, President, and Supreme Court in effect defined not "the exact meaning" but major "constituent elements of the thing we prize so highly," and Lincoln and the lawmakers included blacks in their definition. What follows attempts to sketch some "constituent elements" by reflecting further on aspects of mid-nineteenth century legal culture, our society's "magic mirror."[28]

Over-briefly to state the matter, Lincoln Republicans, including the Radicals, evolved a definition that made an individual's equality before his state's laws the federally enforceable minimum of a reconstructed Union. So justified from history and equity law, nationalized equality fortified federalism and implied short durations for the nation's unaccustomed wartime paternalistic roles.

Justifying equality from history, lawyer Lincoln candidly put Radical cards on the nation's table. At Gettysburg he married patriotism to equality, preaching that "four score and seven years ago (i.e., in 1776) our fathers brought forth . . . a new nation, conceived in Liberty, and dedicated to the proposition that all men are created equal." The Lincoln-Radical thesis reconnected the Declaration of Independence to a future slaveless Constitution. In it, the Declaration redefined "freeitude" in terms of the federal Bill of Rights reconsidered not as a bill of wrongs that the nation must not commit but as a positive authority to the nation to sustain individuals' equal rights against states' wrongs.[29]

The Union's armies took the Lincoln Republicans down this road, in the sense that the Confederacy was never larger than on the first day of the Civil War. Troopers of the initially lily-white Union armies who began contracting Secessia in 1861 and '62 learned quickly to trust only black Southerners, slave and free, as guides, spies, and labor. Self-interested Union soldiers welcomed reinforcements of any skin hue, if only the better to buffer themselves from enemy fire. Lincoln and Congress responded to the soldiers' pragmatic needs and to the conformable political pressures exerted by the soldiers (they voted, unlike Confederate counterparts), their families, and other home front constituents. But Lincoln's pragmatism does not belie the fact that he embraced also the abolitionist lawyers' "critical ethical arguments," in the phrase of law professor-philosopher David Richards.[30]

Emancipation and its linked policies of 1863, the arming of blacks and the reconstructions of thirteen states, were monumental advances in America's history. Armed black bluecoats violated the felony statutes of every slaveholding state. Simple justice required that they, like southern white Unionists, be insulated against retaliations. Ideas gained momentum that federal minimum rights for all states' residents, not only those of the crumpled Confederacy, should inform the postwar Constitution.

Lifelong lawyers as well as politicians, like virtually all attorneys, Lincoln and Taney esteemed state-defined property rights as the guardian of every other right of free Americans. They accepted James Kent's classification "of the right to acquire and enjoy property . . . [as among the] absolute rights of individuals." No state and only rare localities then barred alcohol, abortions, tobacco, drugs, prostitution, pornography, gambling, witchcraft, or other social evils. Governmental interferences with distasteful or even dangerous property rights (known then as civil rights and distinguished from political and social rights) were as unwarranted as arbitrary deprivations of bodily liberty (i.e., civil liberties).[31]

By softening white majorities' views on race relations in a slaveless future, the war eroded these traditionally impregnable legal positions. Abolitionist lawyers accelerated the erosion by applying to inextricably-intertwined race and reconstruction policies concepts from equity law. These concepts stressed the duty of government to encourage self-help—i.e., individuals' opportunity to benefit from their struggles for economic self-sufficiency.

To ease the entrance of white and black Americans into the struggle on roughly equalized terms, a battery of wartime laws institutionalized the early Republican party commitment to free soil and free labor. In monumentally important miscalled nonwar statutes, all without formal racial or gender exclusions and all, like emancipation, unimplementable unless the Union won the war, Congress and President echoed the Northwest Ordinance of 1787. A Homestead law of 1863 greatly enlarged the access of millions of Americans to land, the most basic property of all. Education leading to self-protective voting would result from provisions for federally subsidized institutions of learning, even colleges. And Congress increased the jurisdiction of federal lower courts and numbers of judges so that individuals might protect the fruits of their labor through recourse to law, not to paternalistic welfare institutions. All prefigured major content and purposes of the paramilitary, temporary, and initially budgetless Freedmen's Bureau law of early 1865; all were answers to Lincoln's query of 1862 concerning the rights Americans should enjoy from their nationality.[32]

Lincoln grew to the abolitionist-Radical Republican vision. His role was pivotal in efforts to wed the Declaration of Independence to the Constitution and to recast the offspring, the Bill of Rights, as positive imperatives to federal interventions against state-sanctioned wrongs that demeaned the equality all Americans should enjoy. In his 1858 debates with Stephen Douglas he had insisted daringly that "Liberty is a right inherent and inalienable in men and that herein all men are equal."[33] Then in 1863 Lincoln notified the Union general commanding occupied Louisiana that he "would be glad" if the state included emancipation in a pending constitutional revision and adopted also ". . .some practical system by which the two races could gradually [lift] themselves out of their old relation to each other, and both come out better prepared for the new." The lawyer-President included tax-supported education for blacks in his wish list so that through education they might themselves defend their legal rights to the fruits of their labor.[34]

Extending these ideas to all the seceded states, Lincoln's 1863 Reconstruction proclamation stipulated that they provide for the education of all black residents. Almost simultaneously he also noted happily to Congress the large number of small-holder filings under the Homestead Act by Union Army veterans including Negroes. Though in 1864 he pocket-vetoed the Wade-Davis Bill, Lincoln so valued its provisions for augmented federal court jurisdiction of federally-derived rights issues that he welcomed state reconstructions under its provisions of his own 1863 plan. And in February 1865, Lincoln, with four years ahead in the Presidency, noted that the pending Thirteenth Amendment was gaining majority approval in racist Maryland and Illinois, the latter his native state. The amendment, he stated over-optimistically, ". . .was a very fitting if not an indispensable adjunct to the winding up of the great difficulty . . . [It] is a King's cure for all . . . evils."[35]

Celebrants about Lee's surrender heard Lincoln's April 11, 1865 statement that, acceding to his wishes, Louisianans had reformed their state's constitution, ". . .giving the benefit of public schools equally to black and white, and empowering the Legislature to confer the elective franchise upon the colored man" not only, noteworthily, on Union Army veterans. And, previewing his intentions for all the defeated southern states, Lincoln added: "What has been said of Louisiana will apply generally to other States." Lincoln's public commitment to "nigger citizenship" convinced John Wilkes Booth that assassination was in order.[36] Booth would be tragically successful in frustrating the nation's Lincolnian elevation toward a more decent restored Union.

To sum up, the deserved popular trust that a candid and educable President engendered in watchful voters and Lincoln Republicans' confidence in the capacity of common people to improve their future outmatched Taney's fearful yearnings for a safer past. Released but not divorced from Taney-like static racial and constitutional constraints, under the spurs of prewar abolitionist constitutionalism and wartime patriotism the Lincolnians abandoned rearward-fixated social compact visions of "the Union as it was" that viewed government as enemy. As Peter Hoffer noted recently, "The argument from conscience against the limitations of law led both im-

John Wilkes Booth assassinated President Lincoln on April 14, 1865 at Ford's Theater in Washington, D.C, five days after the Civil War ended.

plicitly and explicitly to an experiment in equitable remedies for the burdens of freedmen and women."[37]

From 1861-64 Taney, many other lawyers, and Democrats generally opposed these evolutions in means, ends, and aspirations. They confirmed persons of static convictions about constitutional and legal rights and race views that a runaway tyranny was in train. Conservatives' views that the Lincoln Republicans' visions for America's near future were unhinged from its past, by 1865 dominated the renascent Democratic party and help to explain Andrew Johnson's successful efforts to blunt progress toward that future. Those efforts brought him to the impeachment. But they would also long deny to millions of black Americans and to all women the equality before law that they desired and deserved.

On May 12, 1866, the abolitionist periodical *The Right Way*, advocated support for the pending Fourteenth Amendment because it implicitly defined national citizenship in terms of the Declaration of Independence and Bill of Rights, and would avoid "reliance . . . upon judicial decisions . . . against freedom." By 1873, however, the Supreme Court's docket would include cases like *Slaughter-House* that mocked hopes of 1865-66, cases that sanctified constitutionally misinterpretations of the Thirteenth and Fourteenth Amendments that denied equal rights to nonwhites and women. By then the American legal community was largely either ignorant about or indifferent to the immoral racial and gender consequences of the Court's aggressively reactionary social role. As an attorney-correspondent of premier constitutionalist Francis Lieber noted: "Lawyers in . . . commercial and industrial communities seldom find application for the principles of ethical and philosophical law which arise out of the relations of government, and their libraries are but scantily supplied with works on these. . .unpractical branches of the law."[38]

Endnotes

[1] Wright, ***The Programme of Peace, by a Democrat of the Old School*** (Boston, 1862), 4.

[2] Relevant literature abounds. One electronic data base, the Expanded Academic Index, lists 190 + war powers titles in 1990-3 alone. Important analyses are in John Norton Moore, "The Justiciability of Challenges to the Use of Military Forces Abroad," 10 ***Virginia Journal of International Law***, 85 (1969). Richard M. Valelly, "War and American National Institutions, 1945 to the Present: The Persistence of Constitutional Crisis?" (Organization of American Historians paper, 1989); Henry B. Cox, ***War, Foreign Affairs, and Constitutional Power, 1829-1901***, (Cambridge, Mass.: Ballinger, 1984); ***The Tethered Presidency: Congressional Restraints on Executive Power***, ed. T. M. Franck (New York: New York University Press, 1981), *passim.*; and Harold Relyea, ***A Brief History of Emergency Powers in the United States: A Working Paper Prepared for the [Senate] Special Committee on National Emergencies and Delegated Emergency Powers***, 93d Cong., 2d sess. Committee Print (Washington, D.C.: GPO, 1974), *passim.*

[3] See John Slonaker, "The U.S. Army and Domestic Disturbances" (Special Bibliography Series 1: Military History Research Collection, Carlisle Barracks, 1970); Francis D. Wormuth and Edwin B. Firmage, eds., ***To Chain the Dog of War: The War Power of Congress in History and Law*** (Dallas: Southern Methodist University Press, 1986), chs. 4, 8-10.

[4] Donald Nieman, "Republicanism, the Confederate Constitution, and the American Constitutional Tradition," in ***An Uncertain Tradition: Constitutionalism and the History of the South***, eds. Kermit L. Hall and James W. Ely, Jr. (Athens, Georgia: University of Georgia Press, 1989), 201-24; Lawrence M. Friedman, "The Law Between the States: Some Thoughts on Southern Legal History," in ***Ambivalent Legacy: A Legal History of the South***, eds. David J. Bodenhamer and James W. Ely, Jr. (Jackson: University of Mississippi Press, 1984), 30-46.

[5] Unsigned review of George S. Williams, ***The Constitution of the United States for the Use of Schools and Academies*** (Cambridge, Mass.: Welch, Bigelow, 1861), in ***North American Review***, XCIV (1862), 271.

[6] ***Messages and Papers of the Presidents***, ed. James D. Richardson (1897), VI, 142, 191. Emphases added. See also Harold M. Hyman, ***A More Perfect Union: The Impact of the Civil War and Reconstruction on the Constitution*** (Boston: Houghton Mifflin, 1975), chs. 3-5.

[7] *Martin v. Mott* 25 U.S. (12 Wheat.) 19, 30 (1827).

[8] *Ex parte Merryman*, 17 Fed. Cas. 144 (C.C.D.Md.) (case No. 9487) (1861); John C. Hurd, ***The Theory of Our National Existence as Shown by the Action of the Government of the United States Since 1861*** (Boston: Little, Brown, 1881), x.

[9] Robert M. Spector, "Lincoln and Taney: A Study in Constitutional Polarization, 15 ***American Journal of Legal History***, 199 (1971); Joseph C. Long, "Ex Parte Merryman: The Showdown Between Two Great Antagonists: Lincoln and Taney," 14 ***South Dakota Law Review***, 207 (1969).

[10] Sophocles, ***Antigone***, eds. David Greene and Richard Lattimore, (New York: Washington Square Press, 1970) 81.

[11] Melvin I. Urofsky, ***A March of Liberty: A Constitutional History of the United States*** (New York: Knopf, 1988), 408.

[12] Horace Binney, ***The Privilege of the Writ of Habeas Corpus Under the Constitution*** 2nd ed., (Philadelphia: C. Sherman, 1862), pp. 37-8. See also Binney to Francis Lieber, Dec. 23, 1861, in *Id.*, unnumbered prefatory page.

[13] Catron to J. M. Carlisle, Feb. 26, 1863, in I ***Legal Historian***, 52 (1958).

[14] *Ex parte Vallandigham*, 68 U.S. (1 Wall.) 243 (1864).

[15] *Luther v. Borden*, 48 U.S. (7 How.) 1 (1849); *Dred Scott v. Sandford*, 60 U.S. (19 How.) 393 (1857); *Dynes v. Hoover*, 61 U.S. (20 How.) 65 (1858). See on *Dynes*, Jonathan Lurie, ***Arming Military Justice: The Origins of the United States Court of Military Appeals 1775-1950*** (Princeton: Princeton University Press, 1992), I, 29-31.

[16] Nelson in *Dred Scott* 60 U.S. (19 How.) at 468. Other data in *Lemmon v. New York*, 20 N.Y. (6 Smith) 562 (1860); Paul Finkelman, "The Nationalization of Slavery: A Counter-Factual Approach to the 1860s," 14 ***Louisiana Studies***, 213 at 221-240 (1975).

[17] Finkelman, "Nationalization," *supra*, note 15 at 231-40; Harold Hyman, "The Narrow Escape From a `Compromise of 1860': Secession and the Constitution," in ***Freedom and Reform: Essays in Honor of Henry Steele Commager***, eds. H. M. Hyman and L. W. Levy (New York: Harper & Row, 1967), 149-66.

[18] Chase to J. D. Van Buren, March 20, 1868, Chase Letterbooks, Ser. 4, Vol. 117, pp. 339-40, Manuscripts Division, Library of Congress.

[19] *Ex parte Stevens* (1861), unreported, is sketched in Urofsky, ***March of Liberty***, *supra*, note 10 at p. 412.

[20] *Ex parte Gordon*, 66 U.S. (1 Black) 503 (1862); [*U.S. v. Gordon*] (C. C. N. D. Ohio 1861 [Unreported]), in Paul Finkelman, ***Slavery in the Courtroom: An Annotated Bibliography of American Cases*** (Washington, D.C.: Library of Congress, 1985), 134-6.

[21] *Prize Cases*, 67 U.S. (2 Black) 635 (1863); *Roosevelt v. Meyer*, 69 U.S. (1 Wall.) 512 (1863); *Ex parte Vallandigham*, 68 U.S. (1 Wall.) 243 (1864).

[22] The Reporter is quoted in 68 U.S. (1 Wall.), xv; *Gelpcke* is at 68 U.S. (1 Wall.) 175 (1864).

[23] First quotation from Charles Bradley, ***The Methods of Changing the Constitutions of the States, Especially that of Rhode Island*** (Boston: Alfred Mudge, 1885), unnumbered preface page; second quote from the title of George Wharton Pepper's pamphlet, ***The Border Land of Federal and State Decisions*** (Philadelphia, 1889).

[24] Unreported, the case is in Richmond, Va., ***Record*** (Sept. 3, 1863); Samuel Tyler, ***Memoir of Roger Brooke Taney*** (Baltimore: John Murphy, 1872), 436-43; Dean G. Acheson, "Roger Brooke Taney: Notes Upon Judicial Self-Restraint," ***Illinois Law Review*** 1 (1937).

[25] Urofsky concluded recently that Lincoln spokesmen were convinced that Americans were peculiarly committed to the idea that except for military matters, broadly defined, all public policies were not only justiciable but also that ". . .key legislation should be tested before the [Supreme] Court to assure that it met constitutional standards, since then it would also have popular support." Urofsky, ***March of Liberty***, *supra*, note 10 at p. 412.

[26] Thomas F. Schwartz, "Salmon P. Chase Critiques ***First Reading of the Emancipation Proclamation of President Lincoln***," 33 ***Civil War History*** 84 at 87 (1987); ***Collected Works of Abraham Lincoln***, ed. Roy P. Basler (New Brunswick, N.J.: Rutgers University Press, 1953), VII, p. 49.

[27] In U.S. Attorney General, ***Opinions***, X, p. 383.

[28] Kermit L. Hall, ***The Magic Mirror: Law in American History*** (New York: Oxford University Press, 1989), chs. 7, 10-12; Harold M. Hyman and William M. Wiecek, ***Equal Justice Under Law: Constitutional Development, 1835-1875*** (New York: Harper & Row, 1982), chs. 2, 9, 10.

[29] Lincoln, ***Collected Works***, *supra*, note 25, VII, pp. 17-23; William Wiecek, ***Sources of Antislavery Constitutionalism in America, 1760-1848*** (Ithaca: Cornell University Press, 1977); Robert Kaczorowski, ***The Politics of Judicial Interpretation: The Federal Courts, Department of Justice, and Civil Rights, 1866-1876*** (New York: Oceana, 1985); Patricia A. Lucie, ***Freedom and Federalism, Congress and Courts, 1861-1866*** (New York: Garland, 1986); Michael K. Curtis, ***No State Shall Abridge: The Fourteenth Amendment and the Bill of Rights*** (Durham: Duke University Press, 1986), all *passim*.

[30] David A.J. Richards, ***Conscience and the Constitution: History, Theory, and Law of the Reconstruction Amendments*** (Princeton: Princeton University Press, 1993), 3, Richard O. Curry, "The Abolitionists and Reconstruction: A Critical Appraisal," 34 ***Journal of Southern History*** 527 (1968).

[31] Kent quoted in James W. Ely, Jr., ***The Guardian of Every Other Right: A Constitutional History of Property Rights*** (New York: Oxford University Press, 1992), 80, and see also chs. 3-4.

[31] Harold M. Hyman, ***American Singularity: The 1787 Northwest Ordinance, the 1862 Homestead and Morrill Acts, and the 1944 G. I. Bill*** (Athens, Georgia: University of Georgia Press, 1986), ch. 2.

[32] Lincoln, ***Collected Works***, III, 1-7.

[33] Lincoln, ***Collected Works***, *supra*, note 25.

[34] *Id.*, VII, 45-56.

[35] William Hanchett, ***The Lincoln Murder Conspiracies*** (Urbana: University of Illinois Press, 1983), 37, 155; Hyman, ***A More Perfect Union***, *supra*, note 6 at 280-1.

[36] Peter Charles Hoffer, ***The Law's Conscience: Equitable Constitutionalism in America*** (Chapel Hill: University of North Carolina, 1990), 124-6. Mark E. Neely, Jr., ***The Last Best Hope of Earth: Abraham Lincoln and the Promise of America*** (1994), *passim*; Louis Gerteis, "The Future of the Freedmen in the United States: Antislavery Expectations for the Postemancipation South," (AHA paper, 1986).

[37] Louis Janin to Lieber, Jan. 16, 1871, Lieber Papers, Huntington Library. On *Slaughter-House*, 83 U.S. (16 Wall.) 36 (1873); on women, *Bradwell v. Illinois* 83 U.S. (16 Wall.) 130 (1873). See also *Minor v. Happersett*, 88 U.S. (21 Wall.) 162 (1875).

The Waite Court And Federal Power To Enforce The Reconstruction Amendments

Earl M. Maltz

In recent years, the proper characterization of the Waite Court has been the subject of considerable scholarly debate. On one hand, commentators such as Robert J. Kaczorowski, Michael Kent Curtis, and Harold M. Hyman and William M. Wiecek have vigorously supported the traditional view of the Waite Court. They argue that the Court's jurisprudence reflected a reactionary vision that was fundamentally hostile to both the rights of free blacks and the vision of federal power that animated the drafters of the Reconstruction Amendments.[1] By contrast, Michael Les Benedict and William E. Nelson have taken a revisionist approach, suggesting that the Waite Court was a relatively moderate institution which made a good faith effort to balance the competing considerations that influenced post-Civil War constitutionalism.[2]

At the risk of oversimplification, I wish to cast my vote with the revisionists. Admittedly, many Waite Court decisions are appropriately cast as constitutionally conservative. However, this pattern was by no means uniform—particularly on the critical question of the extent of the power of Congress to protect free blacks from discrimination. While the Court at times took a narrow view of this power, in other cases it was willing to go beyond the original understanding of the Fourteenth Amendment to vindicate Congressional action.

The first judicial skirmish in the battle over congressional power to protect the civil rights of African-Americans came in *Blyew v. United States*.[3] In *Blyew*, two white men were convicted in federal court for the murder of an African-American woman. The basis for federal jurisdiction was section three of the Civil Rights Act of 1866, which provided for such jurisdiction "of all causes, civil and criminal, affecting persons who are denied or cannot enforce in [state court] any of the rights secured to them by [section one of the statute]." The indictment charged specifically that in Kentucky—the state in which the murder took place—two of the witnesses to the murder would not have been allowed to testify because they were African-American. This was a clear violation of the substantive provisions of the Civil Rights Act.

In the Supreme Court, an attorney retained by the government of the state of Kentucky argued that the Civil Rights Act of 1866 was unconstitutional. The majority of the Court, however, never reached this issue, concluding that the statute by its terms did not grant the federal courts jurisdiction over *Blyew*-type cases. Speaking for the majority, Justice William Strong argued that only the defendants in a criminal trial were persons whose rights were "affected" by the trial within the meaning of the jurisdictional statute. Thus, the mere fact that African-American witnesses were not allowed to testify at such a trial did not provide a sufficient predicate for federal jurisdiction.

Strong's analysis was consistent with the Court's earlier interpretation of similar language in a different context.[4] Nonetheless, his opinion did not draw the support of any of the three Republicans who were to dissent in *The Slaughter-House Cases*.[5] Chief Justice Salmon P. Chase did not participate in *Blyew*, while Justices Joseph P. Bradley and Noah H. Swayne disagreed with the majority's analysis. Speaking for the dissenters,

Joseph P. Bradley (above) was appointed to the Supreme Court in 1870 by President Ulysses S. Grant, along with William Strong. In 1872, Justice Bradley wrote a dissent in *Blyew v. United States*, contending that the federal court did have jurisdiction in the case under the Civil Rights Act of 1866.

Bradley explicitly declined to rest his argument on the exclusion of the live African-American witnesses; indeed, he conceded that in an ordinary civil case, only the parties themselves would be persons "affected" within the meaning of the jurisdictional provision.[6] Instead, he contended that the federal court had jurisdiction because "the cause is one affecting the person murdered, as well as the whole class of persons to which she belonged."[7] Bradley observed that if the victim had been alive, she would have had the right of entering a complaint before a magistrate or the grand jury, and of appearing as a witness at the trial of the offenders. Further, he noted that to deny blacks that right would be a clear violation of the Civil Rights Act.[8] It made no sense, he reasoned, to treat murders differently. Bradley also argued that the jurisdictional provision was fully authorized under the congressional power to remove the "incidents and consequences of slavery, and to instate the freedmen in the full enjoyment of that civil liberty and equality which the abolition of slavery meant."[9]

Bradley's argument suggested a broad reading of congressional enforcement authority. By contrast, despite its significance as an interpretation of the Civil Rights Act of 1866, the majority opinion in *Blyew* left the critical constitutional issues of congressional power undecided. The Court would not begin to address these issues directly until 1875. In the interim, both the jurisprudential and political environments had changed dramatically. On the jurisprudential side, the decision in *Slaughter-House* had sharply limited the scope of the Privileges and Immunities Clause of the Fourteenth Amendment. On the political side, the Republican party had suffered a crushing defeat in the elections of 1874. Both of these events no doubt influenced the decisions in *United States v. Reese*[10] and *United States v. Cruikshank*.[11]

Reese arose from an indictment which was based on sections three and four of the Enforcement Act of 1870. The indictment charged that the defendants had failed, "on account of . . . race and color" to allow an African-American to pay the capitation tax that was a prerequisite to voting, and had also refused to receive the vote of the African-American after being presented an affidavit confirming his willingness to pay the tax. With only one dissent, the Court quashed the indictment. Speaking for seven Justices, Chief Justice Morrison R. Waite gave the relevant sections of the statute an unusually broad interpretation, holding that they were not limited to discrimination based on race or color, but rather prohibited all wrongful refusals to allow a person to qualify to vote.[12] Waite concluded that, thus construed, these sections of the statute went well beyond the power granted to Congress by the Fifteenth Amendment, and as such could not form the basis of a valid indictment.

As the concurrence of Democrat Nathan Clifford[13] and the dissent of Republican Ward Hunt[14] amply demonstrate, Waite's reading of the Enforcement Act was questionable at best. Indeed, during the debates over the Act, Republicans had specifically denied the charge that the proposal reached beyond racial discrimination in state elections.[15] Thus, one is faced with the problem of explaining the decision by Republicans on the Court to adopt such an implausible reading of the Enforcement Act itself. The decision to adopt the broad reading may have represented a tactical retreat in the face of a change in the political climate. Dissatisfaction with the course of Reconstruction had been a significant factor in the Republican electoral reverses in 1874.[16] A decision directly upholding the Enforcement Act could have added fuel to charges that Republicans were bent on indefinitely continuing supervision over the southern electoral process. At the same time, the 1874 defeat made it unlikely that aggressive enforcement action would continue in any event. By adopting the broad reading, the Court avoided the political consequences of upholding the prosecution, while preserving the possibility that a future Congress could intervene on behalf of African-American voters if political circumstances changed.

In any event, proceeding from the premises of the majority, the constitutional limitations that the *Reese* Court imposed on the power of Congress were far from novel. Indeed, they amounted to nothing more than a reaffirmation of the principles of *Minor v. Happersett*[17]—principles that were accepted by many mainstream Republicans during the Reconstruction era.

By contrast, the constitutional issues raised later in the same Term by *Cruikshank* were far more significant. Among the enforcement cases, *Cruikshank* provides the single most complete discussion of the constitutional theory underlying the Court's early interpretation of the Fourteenth Amendment. The case involved a challenge to a series of convictions obtained under section six of the Enforcement Act of 1870—the Pool amendment. The indictment on which the convictions were based charged that the defendants had entered into a conspiracy to deprive two citizens "of African descent and persons of color" of a number of rights. Some of the counts of the indictment were quite general, alleging that because of the race of these citizens, the defendants had conspired to deprive them of the free "exercise and enjoyment of the rights, privileges, immunities, and protection granted and secured to them . . . as citizens of the United States [and the] State of Louisiana" and "'to prevent and hinder them . . . in their several and respective free exercise and enjoyment of every, each, all, and singular the several rights or privileges granted or secured' to them 'by the constitution and laws of the United States.'" Speaking for the Court,[18] Chief Justice Waite found these charges void as a matter of ordinary criminal procedure, concluding that they did not adequately specify *which* "privileges, rights and immunities" were the target of the defendant's allegedly illegal conspiracy.[19] Thus, in his treatment of these counts, Waite was not required to discuss the scope of congressional power to enforce the Reconstruction amendments.

The remaining counts of the indictment did not explicitly charge the defendants with discrimination on the basis of race. They did, however, allege that the defendants had conspired to deprive the named victims of specific rights. Some of the counts asserted that the victims had been hindered and prevented from exercising their right to vote; others cited their right to peaceably assemble and to keep and bear arms. Still others alleged a conspiracy to deprive the victims of their lives and liberty without due process of law. The voting rights allegations were dismissed on the authority of *Reese*;[20] the other counts, by contrast, raised issues of first impression in the Supreme Court.

Waite began his treatment of these issues with a reaffirmation of the *Slaughter-House* distinction between the respective rights associated with state and national citizenship. He then turned to a more general discussion of his view of the nature of American federalism, declaring that "[t]he people of the United States resident within any State are subject to two governments: one State, and the other National; but there need be no conflict between the two. The powers which one possesses, the other does not. They are established for different purposes, and have separate jurisdictions."[21] From a purely theoretical perspective, this vision of state/federal relations was hardly novel; indeed, it formed the basis of Justice Joseph Story's approach to many areas of constitutional law, including the fugitive slave question presented in

A dispute over the 1873 gubernatorial election in Grant Parish, Louisiana, led to the Colfax Massacre—the ambush killing of a group of at least sixty blacks who had seized the Colfax Courthouse. William J. Cruishank was indicted on federal charges of violating the Enforcement Act of 1870. The Supreme Court unanimously ruled that the indictments were faulty.

Prigg v. Pennsylvania.[22] In Story's hands, however, the theory of separate, exclusive spheres of authority was most often used as the basis for circumscribing the power of state governments. For Waite, by contrast, it became an instrument for restricting the scope of *federal* authority under section five of the Fourteenth Amendment.

The breadth of the exclusive authority of state governments was repeatedly emphasized in Waite's treatment of the provisions of the indictment that charged the defendants with incursions on interests protected by the Bill of Rights. His treatment of the Second Amendment right to keep and bear arms and the Fifth Amendment Due Process Clause are particularly significant. Waite argued that the right to keep and bear arms was neither created by the Second Amendment, nor dependent upon the Constitution for its existence; instead, he contended, the Second Amendment simply forbade Congress from infringing upon a pre-existing right. Thus, he concluded that citizens must look to their respective state governments for protection against the violation of this right by their fellow citizens.[23]

Waite viewed the counts charging the defendants with conspiring to deprive citizens of life and liberty without due process as "even more objectionable . . . nothing else than alleging a conspiracy to falsely imprison or murder citizens of the United States." While conceding that the rights to both life and liberty were natural rights, Waite declared that "[t]he very highest duty of the States, when they entered into the Union under the Constitution, was to protect all persons within their boundaries in the enjoyment of these [rights]" and that "[s]overeignty, for this purpose, rests alone with the States." Based on this vision of federalism, Waite drew a sharp distinction between private action, which was left generally to state control, and state action, which the federal government could constitutionally control.[24]

In 1883, the theory that animated the *Cruikshank* Court was extended further in *United States v. Harris*.[25] *Harris* was a challenge to the constitutionality of the Ku Klux Klan Act of 1871. The case arose from an indictment that charged a private conspiracy to prevent a county sheriff from providing the "equal protection of the laws" to several persons who were in his custody. Striking down the indictment for the Court,[26] Justice William B. Woods seemed oblivious to the option of drawing a distinction between private conduct in general and conduct designed to interfere with the processes of state government. Instead, he simply reaffirmed the basic proposition that the Fourteenth Amendment did not vest Congress with the power to reach private action.[27] At the same time, however, Woods clearly left open the possibility that the *Thirteenth* Amendment might be interpreted to allow Congress to punish private, racially-motivated conspiracies to deprive the freed slaves of the rights guaranteed to them by the Reconstruction Amendments. From Woods' perspective, the difficulty with the Ku Klux Klan Act was that, by its terms, it could also be used to punish conspiracies by whites against whites, by blacks against blacks, and by blacks against whites. Thus, since the provisions of the Act were broader than could be authorized by the Thirteenth Amendment, they could not be sustained.[28]

The *Cruikshank* and *Harris* Courts had been careful to leave open the question of whether Congress possessed broad authority to regulate private, racially motivated activity. In 1883, however, even this possibility was largely foreclosed by the decision in the *Civil Rights Cases*.[29] These cases arose from criminal charges against the owners of two hotels and two theaters, respectively, and a civil action against a railroad company. In each case, the gravamen of the allegations was that a patron had been discriminated against on the basis of his race, and that the discrimination violated the Civil Rights Act of 1875.

Speaking for the Court, Justice Bradley treated the owners of the facilities as indistinguishable from other private parties. Bradley did not expressly reject the theory that access to common carriers, inns, and places of amusement was a basic civil right protected by the Fourteenth Amendment. Indeed, one part of his argument conceded the possibility that the Fourteenth Amendment guaranteed such access, and that Congress could require states to enforce the rights of African-Americans in this regard. However, Bradley concluded that Congress lacked authority to act directly against the owners of the facilities themselves. In part, this conclusion rested on a formal argument about the nature of rights themselves.

> . . . [C]ivil rights, such as are guaranteed by the constitution against State aggression, cannot be impaired by the wrongful acts of individuals, unsupported by State authority in the shape of laws, customs, or judicial or executive proceedings. The wrongful act of an individual, unsupported by any such authority, is simply a private wrong, or a crime of that individual; an invasion of the rights of the injured party, it is true . . . but if not sanctioned in some way by the State, or not done under State authority, his rights remain in full force, and may presumably be vindicated by resort to the laws of the State for redress.[30]

He bolstered his argument with a *Cruikshank*-like appeal to the concept of federalism, contending that a contrary position would allow Congress to "establish a code of municipal law regulative of all private rights between man and man in society. It would be to make congress take the place of the State legislatures and to supersede them."[31]

Dissenting, Justice John Marshall Harlan contended that the challenged provisions of the Civil Rights Act were defensible under the enforcement provisions of both the Thirteenth and Fourteenth Amendments.[32] Harlan mounted two major attacks on Bradley's reasoning. First, he contended that Bradley's sharp distinction between governmental action and private action was inapposite to an analysis of the cases before the Court. He emphasized the special status of both public conveyances and inns at common law, as well as the authorities that characterized the right of access to these facilities as an inherent part of the fundamental right to "locomotion."[33] Harlan conceded that places of public amusement stood on a somewhat different footing. Nonetheless, distinguishing *Munn v. Illinois*[34] as a case involving purely private property, he asserted that because these institutions were "established and maintained under direct license of the law" they were "affected with a public interest." For this reason, in Harlan's view, Congress had the power to prohibit places of amusement from discriminating on the basis of race. He reasoned that to hold otherwise would be to allow state governments to "discriminate or authorize discrimination against a particular race, solely because of its former condition of servitude."[35] By linking federal power to the licensing authority, Harlan was able to uphold the statute, while at the same time avoiding the most radical theories of congressional power over private action.

Much of the dissenting opinion, however, was devoted to a more wide-ranging attack on

Bradley's vision of American federalism under the Reconstruction Amendments. Harlan asserted that,

> . . . to hold that the [Fourteenth] [A]mendment remits [the protected rights] to the States for their protection, primarily, and stays the hands of the nation until it is assailed by State laws or State proceedings, is to adjudge that the amendment, so far from enlarging the powers of congress . . . not only curtails them, but reverses the policy which the general government has pursued from its very organization. Such an interpretation of the amendment is a denial to Congress of the power, by appropriate legislation, to enforce one of its provisions.[36]

To support his view that congressional enforcement power under the Fourteenth Amendment should be interpreted broadly, he relied primarily on the general description of the scope of federal power in *McCulloch v. Maryland*[37] and the specific holding in *Prigg*.[38]

The rejection of Harlan's argument—like the earlier decisions in *Cruikshank* and *Harris*—was plainly inconsistent with important elements of theories that were widely shared by congressional Republicans in the early 1870s. At the same time, however, to describe the analysis of the Waite Court as unremittingly conservative would be a mistake. First, despite its emphasis on state autonomy, the decision in the *Civil Rights Cases* did not completely foreclose the federal government from protecting the rights described in the Civil Rights Act of 1875. After noting that all states currently protected those rights, Bradley suggested that Congress could constitutionally require state officials to continue that protection, and punish those officials who failed to do so.[39]

Moreover, Waite's *Cruikshank* opinion strongly suggests that, even where race was not at issue, the Fourteenth Amendment prohibited a significant range of state action. In particular, the implications of *Cruikshank* for the applicability of the Bill of Rights to state action have been somewhat overstated.[40] Admittedly, Waite's opinion does move away from the pure textualist reliance on

Morrison Remick Waite was appointed Chief Justice of the United States in 1874. His service as counsel during the Geneva Arbitration Tribunal helped the United States recover fifteen million dollars from Great Britain over the *Alabama* claims.

the Bill of Rights that marked both the majority and dissenting opinions in *Slaughter-House* and was accepted by even the most conservative members of Congress during the debate over the Civil Rights Act. At the same time, however, *Cruikshank* strongly reaffirmed the principle that the Fourteenth Amendment prevents states from interfering with preexisting fundamental rights, asserting that the Due Process Clause "furnishes an additional guaranty against any encroachment by the States upon the fundamental rights which belong to every citizen as a member of society"[41] and declaring that:

> The equality of the rights of citizens is a principle of republicanism. Every republican government is in duty bound to protect all its citizens in the enjoyment of this principle, if within its power. That duty was originally assumed by the States;

> and it still remains there. *The only obligation resting upon the United States [under the Fourteenth Amendment] is to see that the States do not deny the right. This the amendment guarantees*, but no more.[42]

Rather plainly, Waite viewed rights such as those protected by the First Amendment and the Second Amendment as the kind of fundamental rights that would be protected under this analysis. By contrast, some of the technical requirements codified in the Bill of Rights might not be viewed as rising to the same level of fundamentality; indeed, if the framers of the Fourteenth Amendment had focused specifically on questions such as the rights to indictment by a grand jury prior to trial for a crime, they might plausibly have viewed these matters as less important than the substantive interests protected by other aspects of the first eight amendments. Thus, *Cruikshank* might well be viewed as a precursor of the doctrine of "selective incorporation," as well as the 1884 decision in *Hurtado v. California*,[43] where a majority of the Court rejected the claim that the Fourteenth Amendment incorporated the Fifth Amendment requirement that states obtain grand jury indictments in criminal prosecutions.

Finally, the characterization of the Waite Court as generally hostile to congressional power under the Reconstruction Amendments ignores significant decisions that point in quite the opposite direction. In particular, the Court's treatment of jury discrimination and voting rights cases reflect sympathy for major elements of the Republican theory of federal power.

Discrimination in Jury Selection: *Ex parte Virginia* and *Strauder v. West Virginia*[44]

Ex parte Virginia[45]—the 1879 case in which the Supreme Court dealt with the first challenge to the constitutionality of the Civil Rights Act of 1875—has been largely ignored by scholarly commentators. *Ex parte Virginia* was a petition for a writ of habeas corpus from a state judge who had been indicted for allegedly violating the Civil Rights Act by systematically excluding African-Americans from jury lists that he had prepared. The case raised two analytically distinct problems of federal-state relations. The first was the substantive question of whether the federal government could constitutionally require the states to allow blacks to serve on juries. The second was the institutional question of whether federal law could punish a state official for performance of the duties required of him by state law.

Essentially restating the position taken by Democrats and conservative Republicans in Congress, Justice Stephen J. Field delivered a sharply-worded attack on the constitutionality of the Civil Rights Act.[46] In part, his opinion was based upon the view that the principles of American federalism developed in *Kentucky v. Dennison*[47] and later cases were an absolute bar to direct federal legislative coercion of state officials who were performing official functions.[48] Field declared that "[n]othing . . . could have a greater tendency to destroy the independence and autonomy of the States; reduce them to a humiliating and degrading dependence upon the central government; engender constant irritation; and destroy that domestic tranquility which it was one of the objects of the Constitution to insure."[49]

Field's primary focus, however, was on the claim that the federal government lacked authority to prescribe the qualifications for jurors in state proceedings. After first describing the principle that the federal government is one of enumerated powers,[50] he declared that "if we look into the Constitution, we shall not find a single word, from its opening to its concluding line, nor in any of the amendments in force before the close of the civil war, nor . . . in those subsequently adopted, which authorizes any interference by Congress with the States in the administration of their governments, and the enforcement of their laws with respect to any matter over which jurisdiction was not surrendered to the United States,"[51] and that "[t]o every State . . . there must be, with reference to the subjects over which it has jurisdiction, absolute freedom from all external interference in the exercise of its legislative, judicial, and executive authority."[52]

Stephen J. Field was serving as the chief justice of the California supreme court when he was appointed to the Supreme Court of the United States in 1863. His thirty-four year tenure was the longest in Supreme Court history until William O. Douglas served thirty-six years (1939-1975).

Field then turned specifically to the contention that the Fourteenth Amendment had significantly modified this principle. The essence of his argument was that "a change so radical in the relation between the Federal and State authorities, as would justify legislation interfering with the independent action of the different departments of the State governments, in all matters over which the States retain jurisdiction, was never contemplated by the [Reconstruction] amendments."[53] Drawing on the distinction between civil and political rights, he argued that the right to serve on juries was a political right, and that while the Fourteenth Amendment guaranteed civil rights to all persons, "[it] left to the States to determine to whom the possession of political powers should be intrusted."[54] Field ended his opinion by noting that the Equal Protection Clause—after the decision in *Slaughter-House*, the only plausible source of authority for the Civil Rights Act—applied to both aliens and citizens, and pointing out that the same line of reasoning which supported the result in *Ex parte Virginia* would also seem to require states to allow aliens to serve on juries.[55]

Field, however, was able to gain the vote of only fellow Democrat Nathan Clifford. The seven Republicans on the Court took a quite different view of the impact of the Fourteenth Amendment on the federal structure. William Strong was their spokesman. In sharp contrast to *Slaughter-House* and *Cruikshank*, the majority opinion in *Ex parte Virginia* focused primarily on the nationalizing impact of the amendment. Strong asserted that "[the Reconstruction Amendments are] intended to be, what they really are, limitations of the power of the States and enlargements of the power of Congress,"[56] and that enforcement of the rights guaranteed by the amendments "is no invasion of State sovereignty."[57] While conceding "in the general" that "the selection of jurors for her courts and the administration of her laws belong to each State,"[58] Strong found justification for the Civil Rights Act of 1875 in the flip-side of American federalism—the principle that "in exercising her rights, a State cannot disregard the limitations which the Federal Constitution has applied to her power."[59] Turning to the institutional concern with federal coercion of state officials, Strong contended that "[a] State acts by its legislative, its executive, or its judicial authorities. It can act in no other way. The constitutional provision, therefore, must mean that no agency of the State, or of the officers or agents by whom its powers are exerted, shall deny to any person within its jurisdiction the equal protection of the laws"[60] and concluded that therefore, Congress must have authority to provide penalties for those officials who violate the principles of the Fourteenth Amendment.[61]

Strong focused more specifically with the issue of juries in the companion case of *Strauder v. West Virginia*.[62] *Strauder* dealt with a statute derived from the Civil Rights Acts of 1866 and 1870, which provided for removal of state court actions to federal court by defendants who would be denied or could not enforce a right secured to them by a "law providing for . . . equal rights." In the trial, Strauder, a West Virginia black man, was accused of killing his wife. Under West Virginia state law, only whites were allowed to serve on juries. The defendant claimed that this exclusion was inconsistent with both the Civil Rights Act of 1866 and the Fourteenth Amendment, and that he was therefore entitled to the benefit of the removal provision. The state court denied his motion, and Strauder was convicted of murder. He argued that the state court's refusal to remove the case to federal court vitiated his conviction.

Holding that the case should have been removed, Strong's reasoning tracked the arguments of those who had supported the inclusion of the jury discrimination provision in the Civil Rights Act of 1875. He first contended that "[t]he very fact that [black] people are singled out and expressly denied by a statute all right to participate in the administration of the law, as jurors . . . is practically a brand upon them, affixed by the law, an assertion of their inferiority, and a stimulant to that race prejudice which is an impediment to securing to individuals of the race that equal justice which the law aims to secure to all others."[63] Strong also asserted that the statute denied equal protection to African-American defendants themselves, contending that "[i]t is not easy to comprehend how it can be said that while every white man is entitled to a trial by a jury selected from persons of his own race or color, or, rather, selected without discrimination against his color, and a negro is not, the latter is equally protected by the law with the former."[64]

Many commentators have downplayed the significance of *Ex parte Virginia* and *Strauder*, choosing instead to emphasize the decision in the companion case of *Virginia v. Rives*.[65] Like *Strauder*, *Rives* challenged the refusal of a state court to grant a petition for removal that was based upon a claim that blacks were improperly excluded from a jury in a criminal case. In *Rives*, however, the relevant state statutes did not prohibit African-Americans from serving on juries; instead, the gravamen of the defendant's claim was that the presiding judge made an independent decision to limit jury service to whites, in direct contravention of state law.

Senator Lyman Trumbull was elected to the Senate as a Democrat from Illinois in 1855. However he became a Republican while serving there and a staunch supporter of Abraham Lincoln. He was the author of the Civil Rights Act of 1866. He later rejoined the Democratic party and worked for reform until his death in 1896.

Once again, Strong spoke for the Republican majority. His disposition of *Rives* was strongly influenced by the reformulation of the removal statute during the compilation project that culminated in the passage of the Revised Statutes of 1875. In theory, the purpose of the compilation was only to systematize and clarify existing law; the compilers were instructed not to make substantive changes. Nonetheless, the compilers inexplicably made a major change in the removal provision. As initially formulated in 1866, the provision incorporated by reference the procedures of the Habeas Corpus Suspension Act of 1863, which in turn allowed both pretrial and post-judgment removal—a point clearly reflected in the only systematic exposition of the removal process by Republican Senator Lyman Trumbull of Illinois, the drafter of the Civil Rights Act of 1866.[66] However, the Revised Statutes provided only for pretrial removal. Against this background, the Court unanimously held that removal was not available in *Rives*.

In his majority opinion,[67] Strong noted that the removal statute required a defendant to demonstrate *before trial* that he was unable to enforce his "equal civil rights" in the judicial tribunals of the state.[68] He argued that where (as in *Rives*) state statutes forbade discrimination against African-Americans, one should presume that the defendant could vindicate his rights in either the state trial courts or the state appellate courts.[69] Thus, he concluded, in those cases removal to federal court should not be available.

Rives stands with *Blyew* as a judicial rejection of a facially plausible, expansive reading of the removal jurisdiction. Further, the decision clearly limited the effectiveness of removal as a weapon against discrimination in jury selection. Some commentators have taken these observations a step further, suggesting that *Rives* is simply a further reflection of the Justices' willingness to sacrifice the interests of blacks in order to reinforce both the political settlement of 1877 and the traditional structure of federalism.[70] This argument, however, takes *Rives* out of context. If the members of the Republican majority had in fact been intent on protecting the traditional structure of federalism, they could simply have held that Congress lacked all power to regulate the relevant activity—just as they held only three years later in the *Civil Rights Cases*. Moreover, as Strong's opinion suggests,[71] the threat of criminal sanctions rather than removal was viewed as the main source of protection for the right of African-Americans to be free from state-imposed racial discrimination.[72] Of course, one might still conclude that the Court erred in deciding *Rives* as it did.[73] Nonetheless, to infer that the Republican Justices had no real commitment to eliminating jury discrimination vastly overstates the significance of the decision.

In any event, whatever one's view of *Rives*, *Strauder* and *Ex parte Virginia* radically transformed the theory underlying the Fourteenth Amendment. In drafting the Amendment, the Joint Committee on Reconstruction explicitly rejected a provision that would have barred discrimination in civil rights on the basis of race.[74] Instead, they adopted language that embodied what I have described elsewhere as a principle of limited absolute equality. This principle was not based on the view that, in general, racial discrimination was particularly offensive; rather, it reflected the premise that all men were equally entitled to a fixed set of fundamental rights. As one prominent Republican put it, with respect to natural rights—the rights to life, liberty and property—"it is a question of manhood, not of color."[75] Political rights, such as the right to serve on juries, were not generally viewed as falling within the ambit of limited absolute equality; indeed, during the discussions of the Fourteenth Amendment, Republicans repeatedly and explicitly denied any intention to provide federal guarantees for such rights.[76]

Thus, *Ex parte Virginia* and *Strauder* cannot simply be dismissed as decisions in which, in the words of Benno C. Schmidt, the Court "freed the [F]ourteenth [A]mendment from the narrowest readings of its legislative history and looked for meaning in the . . . broad purposes that the language connoted . . . [and thereby] measure[d] the sweep of equal protection in a functional and broadly historical perspective."[77] Instead, the *Strauder* Court rejected one of the most fundamental premises underlying section one of the Fourteenth Amendment—that the section did not cover political rights.[78] Moreover, the jury discrimination cases rejected the theory of limited absolute equality and were the first to suggest that, at least in some circumstances, race discrimination was itself a matter for special constitutional scrutiny under the Fourteenth Amendment. Finally, in sanctioning the use of criminal penalties against state officials, the Court vindicated the power of Congress to intrude deeply into structure of state governments to enforce the strictures imposed by section one. The jury discrimination decisions thus present a stark contrast to *Cruikshank*, decided only three years earlier, and *Harris* and the *Civil Rights Cases*, both decided within four years after *Ex parte Virginia* and *Strauder*. The unifying principles underlying the Court's actions become clear only when all of these cases are considered together with the 1884 decision in *Ex parte Yarbrough*.[79]

Like *Reese*, *Yarbrough* arose from an indictment which alleged that, in violation of the Enforcement

Act of 1870, a number of private parties had conspired to interfere with the free exercise of the suffrage by an African-American citizen. The indictment in *Yarbrough*, however, differed in one critical respect from that in *Reese*: it specifically alleged that the interference was intended to prevent the citizen from voting in a *federal* election—elections protected separately by the Enforcement Act.

This difference was crucial to the decision in *Yarbrough*. Speaking for a unanimous Court, Justice Miller declared that "[i]f this government is anything more than a mere aggregation of delegated agents of other States and governments, each of which is superior to the general government, [the essence of the state sovereignty heresy] it must have the power to protect the elections on which its existence depends from violence and corruption."[80] Analogizing the Enforcement Act to statutes protecting federal officers in the performance of their duties, Miller declared that "[t]he [constitutional] power in either case arises out of the circumstance that the function in which the party [protected] is engaged or the right which he is about to exercise is dependent on the laws of the United States."[81] He rejected the argument that the right to vote for federal office was simply a function of state law, asserting that Article I, sec. 2 simply adopts state law standards "as the qualification of its own electors for members of Congress."[82]

Samuel Freeman Miller practiced medicine for a decade in Kentucky before moving to Iowa and opening a law practice. Appointed to the Court by President Lincoln in 1862, he served until his death in 1890.

Even if Miller had said no more in *Yarbrough*, the case would have armed Congress with substantial power to protect blacks from private efforts to prevent them from voting. After all, in most cases, those who would attempt to prevent African-Americans from registering would be making no distinction between registration to vote in state and federal elections, and in many instances state and federal elections are held simultaneously. By focusing on the federal element, the federal government could thus constitutionally reach a wide variety of private interference with the electoral process.

Miller, however, went further, seemingly going out of his way to suggest that the Fifteenth Amendment provided Congress with authority to prevent private, racially-motivated interference with the right to vote generally. Distinguishing *Reese*, Miller first analogized the right to vote in federal elections to the Fifteenth Amendment right to be free from racial discrimination in voting rights. He then declared that "[th]e exercise of the right in both instances is guaranteed by the Constitution, and should be kept free and pure by congressional enactments whenever that is necessary."[83]

Miller was clearly aware of the apparent dissonance between the *Yarbrough* analysis and the formalistic definition of rights that had figured so prominently in the *Civil Rights Cases*, decided only a year before. Distinguishing the Fourteenth Amendment state action cases, he asserted that,

> . . . while it may be true that acts which are mere invasions of private rights, which acts have no sanction in the statutes of a State, or which are not committed by any one exercising its authority, are not within the scope of that amendment, it is quite a different matter when Congress undertakes to protect the citizen in the exercise of rights conferred by the Constitution of the United States

essential to the healthy organization of the government itself.[84]

At first glance, the *Yarbrough* decision might seem to reflect a vision of federalism that diverges sharply from the earlier cases describing congressional power to enforce the Reconstruction Amendments. In many respects, however, the parallels between Miller's *Yarbrough* analysis and the approach of the *Cruikshank* Court are striking. Both opinions posit a set of preexisting rights whose protection is remitted to the state governments. At the same time, Congress is viewed as having plenary power to enforce rights whose very existence is derived from the Constitution. Thus, rather than representing a sharp departure from existing doctrine, *Yarbrough* can be viewed as presenting the flip-side of that doctrine.

The Waite Court and the Reconstruction Amendments —A Summary

Taken together, the decisions of the Waite Court reflect a plausible approach to the Reconstruction Amendments. While somewhat more conservative than the theories adopted by most mainstream Republicans in the early 1870s, the Waite Court analysis nonetheless embodied a number of the same themes. On one hand, the goal of Reconstruction had always been to return primary authority over local affairs to state governments. This goal was reflected in *Cruikshank*, *Harris* and the *Civil Rights Cases*. On the other hand, the jury discrimination cases and *Yarbrough* vindicate congressional power to effectuate what became the centerpiece of Republican Reconstruction policy—the maintenance of the right of free blacks to participate in the process of government. Moreover, as *Strauder* and *Ex parte Virginia* demonstrate, the Court was willing to allow Congress to go beyond the original understanding of the Fourteenth Amendment in order to effectuate such rights. Of course, the Justices of the Waite Court might conceivably have chosen a more expansive vision of federal power. Moreover, they could have been more generous in their interpretation of civil rights statutes; their interpretation of the Enforcement Act of 1870 is particularly troubling. However, to dismiss the members of the Waite Court as simple reactionaries would be a grave error; they plainly left open at least the possibility that Congress could act forcefully in defense of the rights of free blacks.

Endnotes

1 Michael Kent Curtis, ***No State Shall Abridge: The Fourteenth Amendment and the Bill of Rights*** (Durham, N.C.: Duke University Press, 1986); Harold M. Hyman and William M. Wiecek, ***Equal Justice Under Law: Constitutional Development, 1835-1875*** (New York: Harper & Row, 1982), ch. 13; Robert J. Kaczorowski, ***The Politics of Judicial Interpretation: the Federal Courts, Department of Justice, and Civil Rights, 1866-1876*** (New York: Oceana, 1985).

2 Michael Les Benedict, "Preserving Federalism: Reconstruction and the Waite Court," in Philip B. Kurland and Gerhard Casper, eds., ***The Supreme Court Review, 1978*** (Chicago: University of Chicago Press, 1979), 39-80; William E. Nelson, ***The Fourteenth Amendment: From Political Principle to Judicial Doctrine*** (Cambridge, Mass.: Harvard University Press, 1988).

3 80 U.S. (13 Wall.) 581 (1872).

4 *United States v. Ortega*, 24 U.S. (11 Wheat.) 467 (1826).

5 83 U.S. (16 Wall.) 36 (1873).

6 *Blyew*, 80 U.S. (13 Wall.) at 598.

7 *Id.*

8 *Id.*, pp. 598-99.

9 *Id.*, p. 601.

10 92 U.S. 214 (1876).

11 92 U.S. 542 (1876).

12 *Ibid.*, pp. 217-20.

13 *Id.*, pp. 222-38.

14 *Id.*, pp. 238-56.

15 ***Congressional Globe***, 41st Cong., 2d Sess. 3663 (1870) (remarks of Sen. Sherman).

16 The campaign of 1874 is described in detail in William Gillette, ***Retreat from Reconstruction: 1869-1879*** (Baton Rouge: Louisiana State University Press, 1979), chs. 9 & 10.

17 88 U.S. (21 Wall.) 162 (1875).

18 Justice Nathan Clifford concurred only in the result. 92 U.S. at 559-69.

19 *Ibid.*, pp. 557-59.

20 *Ibid.*, pp. 555-56.

21 *Ibid.*, p. 550.

22 41 U.S. (16 Pet.) 539 (1842).

[23] *Ibid.*, p. 553.

[24] *Ibid.*

[25] 106 U.S. 629 (1883).

[26] Justice John Marshall Harlan did not reach the merits in *Harris*, concluding that the Court lacked jurisdiction. 106 U.S. 644. However, in *Baldwin v. Franks*, 120 U.S. 678, 698-701 (1887) (Harlan, J., dissenting), Harlan clearly indicated that he believed *Harris* to be wrongly decided.

[27] 106 U.S. at 637-40.

[28] *Ibid.*, pp. 640-41.

[29] 109 U.S. 3 (1883).

[30] *Ibid.*, p. 17.

[31] *Ibid.*, p. 13.

[32] *Ibid.*, pp. 33-57.

[33] *Ibid.*, pp. 41-43.

[34] 94 U.S. 113 (1877).

[35] *Ibid.*, pp. 43-44.

[36] *Ibid.*, p. 51.

[37] *Ibid.*, p. 50.

[38] *Ibid.*, p. 49.

[39] *Ibid.*, p. 25; Michael Les Benedict "Preserving Federalism: Reconstruction and the Waite Court," in Philip B. Kurland and Gerhard Casper, eds., ***The Supreme Court Review, 1978*** (Chicago, 1979), pp. 39-80, at 75-77.

[40] Michael Kent Curtis, ***No State Shall Abridge: The Fourteenth Amendment and the Bill of Rights***, (Durham, N.C. 1984) and Robert C. Palmer, "The Parameters of Constitutional Reconstruction: *Slaughter-House*, *Cruikshank* and the Fourteenth Amendment," ***University of Illinois Law Review***, (1984):739-70, at 762-70, argue that *Cruikshank* held the Bill of Rights to be inapplicable to state governmental action.

[41] *Cruikshank*, 92 U.S. at 554.

[42] *Ibid.*, p. 555 (emphasis added).

[43] 110 U.S. 516 (1884).

[44] The most comprehensive treatment of the jury discrimination cases is Benno C. Schmidt, Jr., "Juries, Jurisdiction and Race Discrimination: The Lost Promise of *Strauder v. West Virginia*," ***Texas Law Review*** 61 (1983):1402-1499, at 1414-55.

Much of the analysis of *Strauder* and *Virginia* in this essay is taken from Earl M. Maltz, "The Civil Rights Act and the Civil Rights Cases: Congress, Court and Constitution," ***Florida Law Review*** 44 (1992):605-635.

[45] 100 U.S. 339 (1879).

[46] *Ibid.*, pp. 349-70 (Field, J., dissenting).

[47] 65 U.S. (How. 24) 163 (1861).

[48] *Ibid.*, pp. 358-60.

[49] *Ibid.*, p. 358. In making this argument, Field relied not only on *Dennison*, but also on *The Collector v. Day*, 78 U.S. (11 Wall.) 113 (1870). In *Day*, the Court held that the principle of state autonomy barred federal taxation of the salary of a state judicial official.

[50] 100 U.S. at 353-57 (Field, J., dissenting).

[51] *Ibid.*, p. 357.

[52] *Ibid.*, p. 362.

[53] *Ibid.*

[54] *Ibid.*, p. 368.

[55] *Ibid.*, pp. 368-69.

[56] *Ibid.*, p. 345.

[57] *Ibid.*, p. 346.

[58] *Ibid.*

[59] *Ibid.*

[60] *Ibid.*, p. 347.

[61] *Ibid.*, p. 348.

[62] 100 U.S. 303 (1879). *Strauder* is discussed in some detail in Schmidt, "Juries, Jurisdiction and Race Discrimination," pp. 1414-33.

[63] *Ibid.*, p. 308.

[64] *Ibid.*, p. 309.

[65] 100 U.S. 313 (1880).

[66] ***Congressional Globe***, 39th Cong., 1st Sess. 1759 (1866).

[67] 100 U.S. at 314-25.

[68] *Ibid.*, pp. 318-19.

[69] *Ibid.*, pp. 320-21.

[70] Harold M. Hyman and William M. Wiecek, ***Equal Justice Under Law: Constitutional Development, 1835-1875*** (New York, 1982), 494-95.

[71] *Ibid.*, p. 321.

[72] ***Congressional Globe***, 39th Cong., 1st Sess. 475 (1866).

[73] Schmidt, "Juries, Jurisdiction and Discrimination," 1433-40, is sharply critical of *Rives* without impugning the motives of the Court.

[74] Benjamin B. Kendrick, ***The Journal of the Joint Committee on Reconstruction, 1865-1867*** (New York, 1914), 106-07.

[75] Quoted in Eric Foner, ***Free Soil, Free Labor, Free Men: The Ideology of the Republican Party Before the Civil War*** (New York, 1970), 290.

[76] These points are discussed in much greater detail in Earl M. Maltz, ***Civil Rights, The Constitution and Congress, 1863-1869*** (Lawrence, KS 1990).

[77] Schmidt, "Juries, Jurisdiction and Race Discrimination," at 1428-29.

[78] Lino A. Graglia, "'Interpreting' the Constitution: Posner on Bork," ***Stanford Law Review*** 44 (1992):1019-50 at 1042, suggests that this distinction was undermined by the adoption of the Fifteenth Amendment. This contention is vastly overstated; the drafters of the Fifteenth

Amendment explicitly rejected broad protection of political rights in favor of the current, narrowly-drawn provision.

[79] 110 U.S. 651 (1884).

[80] *Ibid.*, p. 657

[81] *Ibid.*, p. 662.

[82] *Ibid.*, p. 663.

[83] *Ibid.*, p. 664.

[84] *Ibid.*, p. 666.

Reconstruction: The Civil War Amendments

Michael Les Benedict

The Civil War enhanced the power and reputation of the federal government in general and the presidency and Congress in particular. The Supreme Court, however, had not played a very visible role in the conflict. The *Dred Scott* decision had soiled its reputation, convincing the antislavery Republican party that it had put political and southern sectional interests above the law. Yet Republicans knew that the courts would be crucial in establishing a new, free, constitutional order once the war was over. It was for that reason that Abraham Lincoln had named Salmon P. Chase as Chief Justice. Chase was not only one of the preeminent Republican political leaders, but he had been among the leading legal and constitutional spokesmen of the antislavery movement since the 1840s. The legislation of the Reconstruction era that followed the war enhanced the role of the federal judiciary, and the Supreme Court's role in defining what it meant began the process by which it assumed the central role in the American polity that it plays today. It is ironic that the Court began to expand its role in decisions that claimed to abjure such a role.

The Civil War worked a revolution in American society. It would take more than the space allotted to convey the breadth of the social and economic change occasioned by the abolition of slavery. In legal terms, slaves had been "chattels personal." The law had recognized them primarily as objects—property to be sold, inherited, and used for the convenience or economic benefit of the owner. They had almost no existence as subjects of the law—that is, as legal actors. It was inconceivable in law that a "chattel"—a piece of property—could own property, make a contract, or sue for personal injury. The Thirteenth Amendment abolished the status of slavery everywhere in the United States, converting four million chattel into people. As people, they *were* subjects of the law, but what legal rights would they have?

It is an axiom of American political philosophy that one of the primary purposes of government—if not *the* primary purpose—is to provide protection against private wrongs. Nowadays, we usually think of rights as things protected against government, or sometimes as material entitlements we expect from government. But Englishmen, including those in the American colonies, understood that life, liberty, and property were insecure in the absence of government—in what the great British philosopher John Locke called a "state of nature." People formed governments in order to gain greater security for their natural rights.[1] Americans echoed the common British understanding, so well articulated by Locke, when they wrote in the Declaration of Independence that all men were entitled to unalienable rights and that "[t]o secure these rights Governments are instituted among Men." But under the federal system this obligation to secure rights rested upon the states; it had not been among the powers delegated to the federal government.

In the American system, not only were governments obligated to protect rights from infringement by private individuals, they also were restrained from themselves infringing on rights. The Bill of Rights secured basic civil rights against deprivation by the federal government. But security for civil rights against state deprivation depended almost entirely upon state constitutions, binding on state officials and to be enforced in state rather than federal courts. The exceptions were explicit prohibitions on certain exercises of state power found in Article I, section 10 of the Constitution. No state, the Constitution said, shall, among other things, pass an *ex post facto* law, or a bill of attainder, or impair the obligations of contracts. In effect Article I, sec-

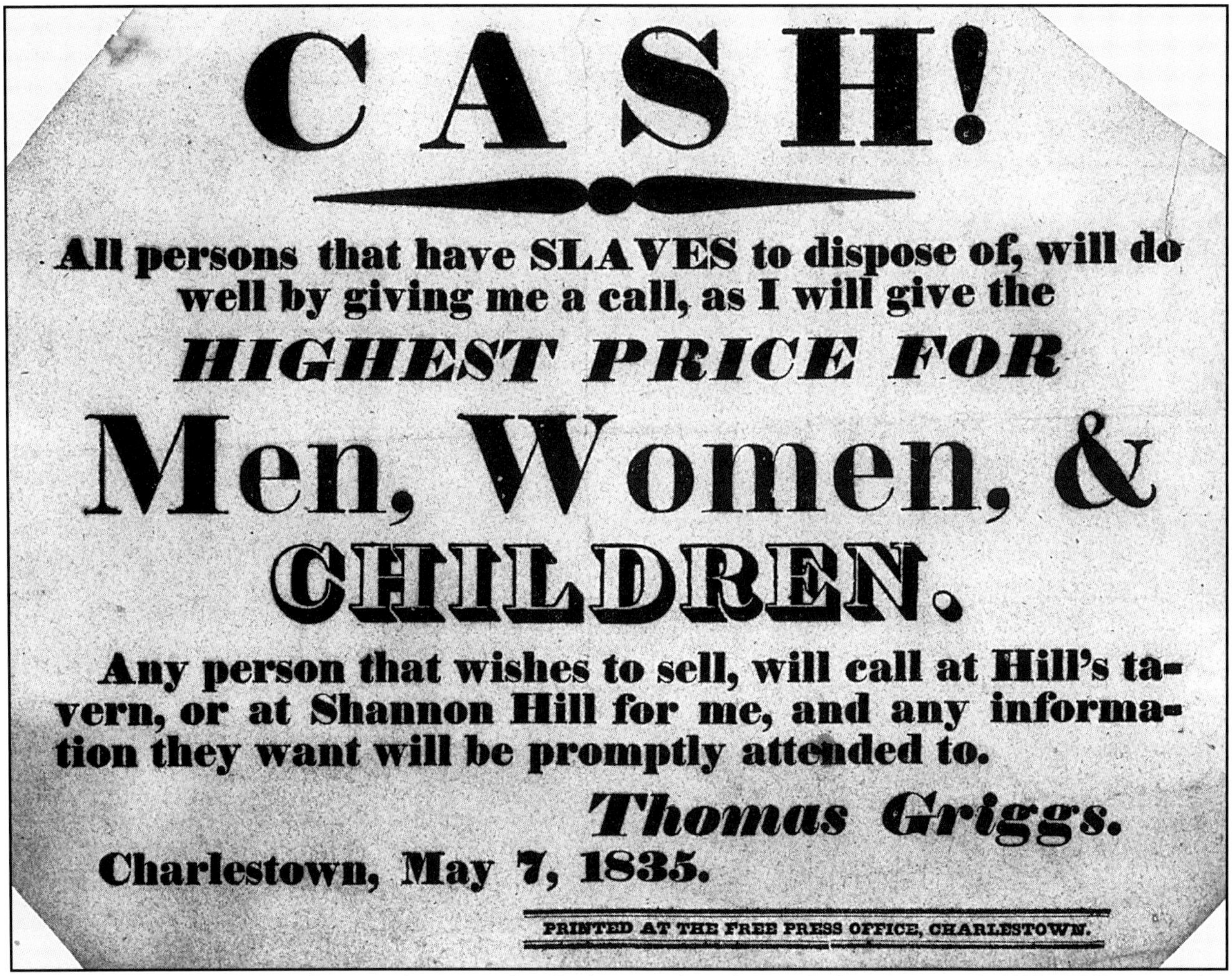

The Constitution prohibited Congress from stopping the importation of slaves before January 1, 1808. While smuggling continued after Congress enacted a ban in 1808, plantation owners concentrated more on slave auctions. Family relations were not always considered by the auctioneer and families were often split as a result of sales.

tion 10 gave people federally secured constitutional rights against state governments, and the Supreme Court of the United States enforced them vigorously. The Constitution also imposed some *obligations* on the states, to which I will return presently.

The slave states offered slaves almost no protection against private wrongs, beyond weak attempts to protect life itself. They conceded no civil rights to slaves at all, denying every right Americans consider fundamental. Slaves could own no property, and therefore, could not buy, sell, devise or inherit it. They could not make contracts, and thus their marriages were not recognized by law, nor their rights to their children. They could not sue or be sued in courts. Strict laws controlled their movements, association, and speech. Except in rare cases, they were not entitled to common-law legal protections when accused of crime.[2]

To sustain the slave system, state governments, both North and South, also limited the rights of free African-Americans to one degree or another. As one would expect, the farther south the state, the greater the restrictions it imposed. The federal government, southern states, and many northern state and local governments excluded free blacks from public facilities and denied them public services. Many northern states and all southern states forbade the entry of free African-Americans from other states. Many northern states limited black access to the courts; in the southern states and the federal courts access was severely restricted. Southern states passed laws limiting free blacks' freedom of movement, controlling their ability to associate, forbidding them to enter professions, and obstructing their entry into various nonprofessional occupations. Many southern states required freed slaves to leave on pain of reenslavement. No state outside New England permitted its African-American citizens to vote or hold governmental office, and this meant none could serve on juries, since potential jurors were drawn from voting rolls.[3]

Southern states also circumscribed the rights of white citizens, especially the rights of freedom of speech and of the press that could be used to criticize slavery publicly. United States postmasters accepted and approved state laws barring antislavery literature from the southern mail. Antislavery spokesmen could expect no protection from southern governments if they traveled South, and they dared not bring their message to the South in person. In the North they were subjected to officially-inspired violence.[4]

Before the war most of these matters were conceded to be within state jurisdiction. If they raised questions of civil liberty, those questions had to be resolved in state forums. The Constitution delegated no direct authority to the federal government over them. None of them violated the explicit prohibitions of Article I, section 10. As I mentioned earlier, the Constitution did impose some obligations upon the states, primarily in Article IV. Besides having to return fugitives from justice and fugitives from labor—that is, runaway slaves—states were to give full faith and credit to the legal acts of other states. Moreover, Article IV declared that the citizens of every state should have the privileges and immunities of citizens in the several states, confusing language that might mean that the states were obliged to give visiting citizens from other states the same rights as their own citizens, or which might mean that all states were obliged to honor the fundamental rights accorded American citizens generally. But did these constitutional obligations create enforceable prohibitions to counteract states if they tried to evade their responsibility? Did they authorize federal action to remedy evasions?

Although the Supreme Court held that the federal government was authorized to enforce the Fugitive Slave Clause of Article IV,[5] most jurisprudents held that neither the federal courts nor Congress had the power to enforce the Privileges and Immunities Clause, because it did not specifically state that "No state shall deprive citizens of privileges and immunities," in language similar to that of Article I, section 10.[6] The Supreme Court seemed to sustain this view when it ruled that the Bill of Rights limited only the federal government and not the state governments, in part because the amendments that constituted the Bill of Rights did not specifically say "No state shall" deprive or impair the rights they listed.[7] On the eve of the Civil War in 1860 the Supreme Court directly held that it lacked the power to force a state to meet its obligation to return fugitives from justice.[8] And partly to make sure that the Privileges and Immunities clause could not be used to protect the rights of African-Americans, in the *Dred Scott* case the Court ruled that Negroes were not citizens of the United States even if they were recognized as citizens of individual states.[9]

That was the situation in 1865 as the war ended. The states were in the process of ratifying the Thirteenth Amendment, which banned slavery. The Amendment also authorized the federal government to pass "appropriate legislation" to enforce it. But did that include legislation to define and protect the rights of the freedpeople? Most Republicans believed that it did, and in 1866 they passed a Civil Rights Act declaring all persons born in the United States to be citizens, except tribal Indians, and requiring all states to secure the same basic rights to all their residents that they secured to their white residents.[10] The same law made the federal courts the prime engines of its enforcement, authorizing anyone deprived of these rights to transfer his or her case directly to the local federal courts rather than having to appeal all the way through the state court system and then to the Supreme Court of the United States.

In part to assure the constitutionality of such legislation, the Republicans passed the Fourteenth Amendment. Its first section again declared all persons born in the United States citizens, except tribal Indians, and defined their rights in more general language than that of the Civil Rights Act. And this time—to make federal power to protect rights absolutely clear—they used the critical language of state limitation. The Fourteenth Amendment declares, "No state shall make or enforce any law which shall abridge the privileges or immunities of citizens of the United States; nor shall any State deprive any person of life, liberty, or property, without due process of law; nor deny to any person within its jurisdiction the equal protection of the laws." This clearly authorized the federal courts to enforce the limitations just as they did other specific constitutional limitations upon the states. In later years the chief author of the language, Representative John A. Bingham of Ohio, explained that this was exactly why he used the "No state shall" formulation.[11] Moreover, the last section of the Amendment authorized Congress to enforce it with appropriate legislation. Three years later Congress sent the Fifteenth Amendment to the states. It forbade state and federal governments from imposing any racial test for voting. Both amendments authorized Congress to enforce them with appropriate legislation. After their ratification, Congress did so, among other things repassing the Civil Rights Act, and again making immediate removal of cases to the federal courts a prime mechanism of enforcement.

These constitutional changes reflected an immense social and economic revolution. But the constitutional changes themselves were both radical and conservative. They were radical in so far as they conferred on the federal government—both the courts and Congress—the power to protect the rights of American citizens. But they were conservative in the sense that Congress clearly hoped to accomplish this goal within the framework of the traditional federal system. The obligation to protect people from private wrongs remained with the states. Was it now enforceable? Perhaps. That would depend on the interpretation given the Equal Protection Clause of the Fourteenth Amendment. Did it mean that states must offer full protection and that such protection must be equal, or did it mean only that whatever protections states did provide had to be provided equally to all? But even under the broader understanding, the "No state shall" language meant that states retained the primary authority to deal with day-to-day relations among their citizens and were the primary source of their protection. Only when states failed to protect rights or actively infringed on them would the Fourteenth and Fifteenth Amendments come into play. The Fifteenth Amendment was designed primarily to encourage the southern states to meet their obligations by enabling African-Americans to put political pressure on their officials. As Republicans consistently stated, there would be no necessity for federal action—no practical change in the operations of the federal system at all—if states simply met their obligations to protect fundamental rights equally.[12]

Moreover, the Republicans deliberately avoided the alternative of specifically and expressly protecting the rights of African-Americans. The slavery system had circumscribed the rights of whites as well as blacks, and Republicans meant to secure the basic rights of both. In addition, Republicans did not want to be politically vulnerable to the charge of legislating only for the benefit of black people. Thus the Fourteenth Amendment and the laws that enforced it made no reference to color.[13]

The language of the Fourteenth Amendment was general and ambiguous. It echoed the Privileges and Immunities Clause of Article IV and the Due Process Clause of the Fifth Amendment. The Equal Protection Clause resonated with Jacksonian anti-monopoly, anti-special privilege rhetoric. But precise definitions were not part of the national debate that culminated in the Amendment's ratification. Ultimately the Supreme Court would have to define what the general words of the Fourteenth Amendment meant and the scope and extent of federal enforcement authority.[14]

The Court has been severely criticized for defining the Amendments in ways that limited the ability of the federal government to protect civil and political rights. The dominant view among historians and legal scholars has been that the Court subverted the intention of Congress and perverted the meaning of the Fourteenth Amendment.[15] However, the situation is not that simple. The Republicans who had framed the Fourteenth Amendment desired to do so within the federal system. They sought to impose nationally enforceable limits on state power to infringe rights. They intended to apply pressure forcing states to fulfill their duty to protect, but they did not want to shift the primary duty to protect individuals from the wrongful acts of others to the national government. The "No state shall" language reflected their intentions exactly. It converted the unenforceable obligation of the old Privileges and Immunities Clause of Article IV into an enforceable prohibition. It also left the states with the same general jurisdiction over daily relations among their residents that they had always had.

But despite these efforts, actual cases made clear that the Fourteenth Amendment, had the potential radically to alter the federal system. This was all too clear in the first important Fourteenth Amendment case to reach the Supreme Court. The plaintiffs in *The Slaughter-House Cases* of 1873[16] were not African-Americans but white butchers from New Orleans, challenging a Louisiana law, passed by the black-supported Republican government of the state. It required all slaughtering of animals to be undertaken in a single slaughterhouse, built and owned by a state-chartered private monopoly. The purpose of the law was to protect public health by barring butchers from slaughtering animals on whatever premises they happened to own, in an era before refrigeration and modern sanitation. The monopoly was granted in exchange for private sponsorship of the building and operation of the slaughterhouse at a time when southern governments were strapped for cash. If the Supreme Court accepted the case for decision, much less agreed that the law deprived the butchers of the privileges and immunities of American citizenship, every state health law would be subject to a similar challenge. Moreover, since the Amendment authorized congressional as well as judicial enforcement, such a challenge could be carried to Congress as well, subjecting to Congressional reversal every state law that might be construed to infringe a right.

Was that what Republicans had intended in passing the Fourteenth Amendment? Obviously not. In avoiding that result, however, the Court interpreted the Fourteenth Amendment's Privileges and Immunities Clause so narrowly and perversely as to render it almost meaningless. The Amendment implicitly distinguished privileges and immunities associated with national citizenship from those associated with state citizenship, the

The Fifteenth Amendment to the Constitution was ratified in 1870, guaranteeing that the right of citizens to vote shall not be denied or abridged "on account of race, color, or previous condition of servitude." In the first elections following ratification, five Southern states sent African-Americans to Congress. However, once Reconstruction ended, several of the Southern states adopted poll taxes, literacy tests, and other impediments to the voting rights of African-Americans.

Court insisted. The Amendment merely forbade states from infringing the former, which included only rights pertaining to one's relations to the national government. It left the states in complete control of rights related to the areas where they traditionally had exercised jurisdiction. Obviously that was not what the Republicans had intended either. But the Court's goal was to avoid a radical expansion of federal judicial and congressional power into nonracial public policy, not to undermine black rights. On the contrary, the Court insisted that the sole purpose of the Fourteenth Amendment was to protect the former slaves—thus injecting the very racial purpose into the Amendment that Republicans had sought to avoid.

Statutory provisions challenged in *U.S. v. Cruikshank*,[17] *U.S. v. Reese*,[18] *U.S. v. Harris*,[19] and the *Civil Rights Cases*[20] acted directly on private individuals, irrespective of state action or dereliction (although in the *Reese* case the provision—along with another that did specify state action—was brought to bear on election officials). *Cruikshank* was a prosecution of private individuals for depriving people of rights specified in the Bill of Rights, such as the right to associate and bear arms, and of due process of law and equal protection generally. *Reese*, a prosecution for interfering with the right to vote in state elections, was brought under a provision that did not clearly require a racial motivation for conviction. *Harris* was a prosecution of a lynch mob for depriving their victims of the equal protection of the laws. The *Civil Rights Cases* involved criminal prosecutions and a civil action for damages under the Civil Rights Act of 1875, which forbade private individuals from denying equal accommodations on racial grounds, without requiring any allegation of state support.

To sustain these prosecutions would be to recognize Congress's direct, primary authority to define and protect the individual rights of all Americans, irrespective of state action. Again the Supreme Court refrained from doing so, preserving the federal system at the expense of effective protection of civil and political rights. It held the indictments defective in the *Cruikshank* case and the provisions of the law unconstitutional in *Reese*, *Harris*, and the *Civil Rights Cases*.

From the *Cruikshank* and *Civil Rights Cases* there emerged the well-known "state-action doctrine." The "No state shall" language, incorporated into the Fourteenth Amendment to assure that the restriction it imposed on the states would be enforceable, now was interpreted as a limitation on the power of Congress. Because of that language, "the first section of the Fourteenth Amendment . . . is . . . prohibitory upon the States," the Court declared. "Individual invasion of individual rights is not the subject-matter of the amendment." The Fourteenth Amendment authorized Congress only to pass legislation to counteract such prohibited state action. "This is the legislative power conferred upon Congress, and this is the whole of it." The Fourteenth Amendment "does not invest Congress with power. . . to create a code of municipal law for the regulation of private rights . . . ."[21]

In imposing the state-action rule, the Supreme Court adhered to Congress's commitment to preserving the states' primary responsibility for protecting the rights of individuals against private wrongs. Yet the Court's language seemed to preclude federal action even if the states failed to meet that responsibility. It seemed to preclude a "state *in*action rule" that would have permitted Congress to provide protection against private wrongs when states failed to do so. In interpreting the states' obligation to provide "equal protection," the Court stressed equality rather than protection.[22]

It is the state-action doctrine and the *Slaughter-House Cases*' narrow definition of the Privileges and Immunities Clause for which the Reconstruction-era Supreme Court is best remembered. Both limited federal power to protect rights. Less known—indeed almost forgotten—were the Justices' *dicta*, articulated especially in their circuit court cases, that recognized broader congressional power. Congress could intervene only against state action to secure due process and equal protection in general. But the Justices indicated that Congress could protect *basic* civil rights against even private infringement—not through the authority delegated by the Fourteenth Amendment but rather under the authority of the Thirteenth on the ground that the deprivation of such basic rights was among the incidents of slavery.[23] On circuit, Justice Joseph P. Bradley made clear his view that the Fifteenth Amendment authorized the federal government to punish the efforts of private individuals to deny citizens the right to vote irrespective of race.[24] Although the Court was never so explicit, it did not rule laws aimed at conspiracies to hinder voting unconstitutional on state-action grounds. Instead, both Bradley on circuit and the Court as a whole insisted that any statute enforcing the Fifteenth Amendment specify racial motivation as an element of an offense.[25]

But just as the Justices limited the powers delegated by the Fourteenth Amendment, they tried to restrict the scope of the power to punish private action that they recognized under the Thirteenth and Fifteenth Amendments. In the case of the latter, it was the right to vote regardless of race that might be protected, not the right to vote generally. Therefore, the Amendment required an allegation that any private or state deprivation of the right to vote was motivated by the race of the victim. With regard to the Thirteenth Amendment, it was the incidents of slavery that were subject to congressional action. Not only were these defined to refer to the deprivation of the most fundamental rights, but, the Justices concluded, the Thirteenth Amendment implied the necessity of a racial motivation as well.[26] Once again, in order to contain the potential for expansive interpretation in the post-Civil War amendments, the Court stressed their racial aspects.

As a matter of law, the Courts' opinions in these cases—and other cases, where the Justices sustained prosecutions under civil and political rights laws[27]—left far-reaching power in the federal government to protect rights.[28] But the practical consequences of these decisions were tragic for African-Americans, and indeed for the history of our country. Southern Democrats and their northern allies seized upon the decisions to attack the constitutionality of the entire rights-protection effort. Southern terrorists were encouraged; law-enforcement officers were demoralized.

Had the Court repudiated the clear meaning of the Fourteenth Amendment? No, because there *was* no clear meaning of the Fourteenth Amendment. Did the Court repudiate the spirit of the Amendment? In part yes, in part no. Republicans had sought to preserve federalism and protect the rights of African-Americans. When the two came into conflict, they opted to protect civil rights in the manner that was least damaging to federalism. The Justices opted to protect federalism at the expense of rights. This choice is not readily accepted by modern analysts, who are deeply committed to civil liberty in an age accustomed to the exercise of wide-ranging national power in a radically different economic and social environment. Nonetheless, the policy results of judicial enforcement of the Civil War Amendments were more a consequence of the limits that Republican support for federalism placed on their Reconstruction program, than a repudiation of that program.

For all their desire to preserve the federal system, the Republicans had fashioned civil rights legislation and constitutional amendments that potentially authorized the exercise of a degree of federal power ahead of its time. The full potential of the change became apparent only as the Justices faced actual cases and considered the legal consequences of the precedents they would set if they interpreted the amendments and enforcement laws generously. They quailed before those consequences and tried to contain them, while at the same time preserving the national government's power to protect basic civil and political rights. They failed largely because succeeding Justices of the Supreme Court, indifferent to protecting African-American rights, seized on the elements of their opinions that constricted federal power and limited the scope of rights protected by the Constitution. The Reconstruction Court's more generous statements of federal power were ignored.

It was not until the nationalization of the American economy in the twentieth century, when almost all commerce became interstate and foreign commerce, that the federal power that was potential in the United States Constitution became real. A revolution in the federal system occurred, making possible the exercise of powers over local government and private individuals in ways that seemed aberrant in the Civil War era. If the Supreme Court helped circumscribe the effect of the Fourteenth and Fifteenth Amendments after the Civil War, it played a critical role in revitalizing the Amendments after the revolution in federalism made it possible to do so.

Endnotes

[1] John Locke, ***The Second Treatise of Government***, chaps. 1-2, 7-10 in Locke, ***Two Treatises of Government***, ed. Peter Laslett (rev. ed., Cambridge, Eng.: Cambridge University Press, 1963), 307-26, 361-400.

[2] The standard study of slaves' legal status remains Kenneth M. Stampp, ***The Peculiar Institution: Slavery in the Ante-Bellum South*** (New York: Alfred A. Knopf, 1956), 141-91. In the rare cases when slaves accused of crimes were brought before the regular courts, they were sometimes afforded basic common-law protections, especially in capital cases. Daniel J. Flanigan, "Criminal Procedure in Slave Trials in the Antebellum South," 40 ***Journal of Southern History*** 537-64 (1974); A.E. Keir Nash, "A More Equitable Past? Southern Supreme Courts and the Protection of the Ante-

bellum Negro," 48 ***North Carolina Law Review***, 197-242 (1970); Nash, "Reason of Slavery: Understanding the Judicial Role in the Peculiar Institution," 32 ***Vanderbilt Law Review***, 7-218 (1979). Mark Tushnet, ***The American Law of Slavery 1810-1860: Considerations of Humanity and Interest*** (Princeton: Princeton University Press, 1981) argues that southern judges were torn between treating slaves as human beings within a system of social relations and property within an economic system. However, his book confirms that in neither case were slaves accorded legal rights.

[3] The standard studies remain Leon Litwack, ***North of Slavery: The Negro in the Free States, 1790-1860*** (Chicago: University of Chicago Press, 1961) and Ira Berlin, ***Slaves Without Masters: The Free Negro in the Ante Bellum South*** (New York: Pantheon, 1974).

[4] Clement Eaton, ***The Freedom-of-Thought Struggle in the Old South*** (Durham, N.C.: Duke University Press, 1940); Russel B. Nye, ***Fettered Freedom: Civil Liberties and the Slavery Controversy 1830-1860*** (East Lansing: Michigan State University Press, 1949); Leonard L. Richards, ***"Gentlemen of Property and Standing": Anti-Abolition Mobs in Jacksonian America*** (New York: Oxford University Press, 1970).

[5] *Prigg v. Pennsylvania*, 41 U.S. (16 Pet.) 539 (1842); *Ableman v. Booth*, 62 U.S. (21 How.) 506 (1859).

[6] Richard L. Aynes, "On Misreading John Bingham and the Fourteenth Amendment," 103 ***Yale Law Journal***, 57-104, at 91, 74-77, 83-94 *passim* (1993).

[7] *Barron v. Baltimore*, 32 U.S. (7 Pet.) 243 (1833).

[8] *Kentucky v. Dennison*, 65 U.S. (24 How.) 66 (1861).

[9] *Dred Scott v. Sandford*, 60 U.S. (19 How.) 393 (1857).

[10] ***U.S. Statutes at Large***, 14 (1865-1867): 27-29.

[11] Bingham in the ***Congressional Globe***, 42 Cong., 1 Sess, Appendix, 84 (Mar. 31, 1871).

[12] Michael Les Benedict, "Preserving the Constitution: The Conservative Basis of Radical Reconstruction," 61 ***Journal of American History***, 65-90 (1974). But *see* Robert J. Kaczorowski, "To Begin the Nation Anew: Congress, Citizenship, and Civil Rights after the Civil War," 92 ***American Historical Review***, 45-68 (1987).

[13] For example, section 6 of the Enforcement Act of 1870 read: "That if two or more persons shall band or conspire together . . . to injure, oppress, threaten, or intimidate any citizen with intent to prevent or hinder his free exercise and enjoyment of any right or privilege granted or secured to him by the Constitution or laws of the United States, or because of his having exercised the same, such persons shall be held guilty of felony . . . ." ***U.S. Statutes at Large***, 16 (1869-71): 141.

[14] It is because congressmen did not define the meaning of the Fourteenth Amendment with precision that there has been so much controversy over the original understanding of its terms. For the best discussion of the vagueness of the widely accepted generalities that went into the Fourteenth Amendment, *see* William E. Nelson, ***The Fourteenth Amendment: From Political Principle to Judicial Doctrine*** (Cambridge, Mass.: Harvard University Press, 1988).

[15] Classic statements of the dominant view are Carter G. Woodson, "Fifty Years of Negro Citizenship as Qualified by the United States Supreme Court," 6 ***Journal of Negro History***, 1-53 (1921); Eugene Gressman, "The Unhappy History of Civil Rights Legislation," 50 ***Michigan Law Review***, 1323-58 (1952); Robert J. Harris, ***The Quest for Equality: The Constitution, Congress and the Supreme Court*** (Baton Rouge: Louisiana State University Press, 1960), 58, 82-91; Rayford Logan, ***The Betrayal of the Negro: from Rutherford B. Hayes to Woodrow Wilson*** (rev. ed., New York: Collier Books, 1965), 105-24; Loren Miller, ***The Petitioners: The Story of the Supreme Court of the United States and the Negro*** (New York: Pantheon, 1966), 85-164. The present standard interpretation of judicial interpretation of Reconstruction-era legislation takes the same view. Robert J. Kaczorowski, ***The Politics of Judicial Interpretation: The Federal Courts, Department of Justice and Civil Rights, 1866-1876*** (New York: Oceana, 1985).

[16] *Slaughter-House Cases*, 83 U.S. (16 Wall.) 36 (1873).

[17] 92 U.S. 542 (1876).

[18] 92 U.S. 214 (1876).

[19] 106 U.S. 629 (1883).

[20] 109 U.S. 3 (1883).

[21] *Civil Rights Cases*, at 10-11.

[22] There were both explicit and implicit indications that various Justices did believe that state inaction justified congressional action. However, the language was more explicit in circuit court than Supreme Court opinions, and language forcefully manifesting commitment to state-centered federalism made a greater impression upon contemporaries. *See* Benedict, "Preserving Federalism," 66-67 for a discussion of state inaction and Laurent B. Frantz, "Congressional Power to Enforce the Fourteenth Amendment against Private Acts," 73 ***Yale Law Journal***, 1353-84 (1964) for a legal argument that the Court had endorsed a state-inaction rule.

[23] *Civil Rights Cases*, 109 U.S. at 23. By the time he wrote the opinion in the *Civil Rights Cases*, however, Justice Bradley seems to have retreated somewhat from his most explicit statement of this understanding. He seemed at pains to point out the state-action orientation even of the Civil Rights Act of 1866, which was originally passed under the authority of the Thirteenth Amendment. *Id.*, at 16-17. In his circuit court opinion in *Cruikshank*, he stated his conviction that the Thirteenth Amendment reached private action infringing basic rights much more forcefully, using the Civil Rights Act to demonstrate the power. *U.S. v. Cruikshank*, 25 F. Cas. 707, at 711 (C.C.D. La.) (Case No. 14,897).

[24] *Id.*, at 713.

[25] *Id.*, at 715, *U.S. v. Reese*, 92 U.S. 214 (1876); *U.S. v. Harris*, 106 U.S. 629 (1883).

[26] *U.S. v. Cruikshank*, 25 F. Cas. at 711-12; *U.S. v. Harris*, at 640-41. *See* Michael Les Benedict, "Preserving Federalism: Reconstruction and the Waite Court," 1978 ***Supreme Court Review*** 39-79.

[27] *Ex parte Clarke*, 100 U.S. 199 (1880); *Strauder v. West Virginia*, 100 U.S. 303 (1880); *Virginia v. Rives*, 100 U.S. 313 (1880); *Ex parte Virginia*, 100 U.S. 339 (1880); *Ex parte Siebold*, 100 U.S. 371 (1880); *Ex parte Yarbrough*, 110 U.S. 651 (1884).

[28] Michael Les Benedict, "Preserving Federalism"; Benedict, "'Judicial Infamy': The Black Testimony Cases," in A.E. Dick Howard and Melvin I. Urofsky (eds.), ***Virginia and the Constitution*** (Charlottesville: Virginia Commission on the Bicentennial of the United States Constitution, 1992), 53-82.

Reconstruction, The Waite Court, and the Politics of History

Randall Kennedy

The history of the Supreme Court's early interpretations of the Reconstruction Amendments has been the focus of intense, often, acrimonious, debate. The intensity derives in part from the momentousness of the subjects at issue. One of the subjects is the relationship of the states to the federal government. No one seriously contends that federalism was left untouched by the Civil War and Reconstruction. Fighting erupts, however, over differing claims regarding the extent to which the authority of the states was subordinated by the Reconstruction Amendments to the authority of the national government. A second explosive subject, closely related to the first, is the legal status of the African-American. No one seriously doubts that the Thirteenth Amendment abolished slavery, or that the Fourteenth Amendment, overruling *Dred Scott v. Sandford*, enabled native born blacks to become citizens of the United States entitled to the equal protection of the laws, or that the Fifteenth Amendment prohibited the states from excluding persons from the ballot on account of race. But dissension surrounds other issues that hinge on the meaning of those amendments. For instance, properly read, does the Fourteenth Amendment, permit, compel, or prohibit beneficial affirmative action on behalf of African-Americans?

A second reason that competing interpretations of the Supreme Court's early encounters with the Reconstruction Amendments have generated an unusual degree of intensity is suggested by the contemporary relevance of the question noted immediately above. For the interpretation of the Court's performance is of more than scholarly concern; winning and losing in these historiographical struggles affect current policies that touch all Americans. Controversy surrounds the role that original intent and precedent should play in judicial decision-making. The notion, however, that some weight ought to be given to the original intent of the framers of the constitutional amendments and the

The first Justice John Marshall Harlan dissented in the *Civil Rights Cases* because he believed that the majority of the Court was interpreting the Reconstruction Amendments too narrowly.

Supreme Court's precedents is sufficiently influential to make constitutional and Supreme Court history a matter of ongoing and urgent concern.

For many, the history of the Supreme Court's early interpretations of the Reconstruction Amendments is a two-chapter story of tragic betrayal. In chapter one, the Reconstruction Amendments make overdue but nonetheless grand promises that henceforth the federal government would guarantee racial equality. In chapter two, the Supreme Court undermines those promises by construing them too narrowly, thereby depriving the federal government of authority bestowed upon it by the framers of the Reconstruction Amendments. An early version of this pejorative portrayal was offered by Justice John Marshall Harlan in his dissent in the *Civil Rights Cases*.[1] Objecting to the Court's ruling that the public accommodations section of the Civil Rights Act of 1875 was beyond the powers granted to the Congress by the Reconstruction Amendments, Justice Harlan complained that "the substance and spirit of the recent amendments of the Constitution have been sacrificed by a subtle and ingenious verbal criticism . . . . Constitutional provisions, adopted in the interests of liberty, and for the purpose of securing, through national legislation, if need be, rights inhering in a state of freedom, and belonging to American citizenship, have been so construed as to defeat the ends the people desired to accomplish, and which they supposed they had accomplished by changes in their fundamental law."[2] A later version of this story was told by, among others, Carter G. Woodson and Loren Miller. Similarly, bewailing the Supreme Court's "betrayal" of the Reconstruction Amendments and the federal laws enacted pursuant to those constitutional promises, Eugene Gressman asserted in "The Unhappy History of Civil Rights Legislation"[3] that "seldom, if ever have the power and the purpose of legislation been rendered so impotent." This story, he declared, "constitutes one of the saddest chapters in the historic struggle to effectuate the American ideal of freedom and equality for all."

The villains of the story were the majority of Justices who comprised the Court presided over by Morrison R. Waite between 1874-1888, the Justices who handed down *The Slaughter-House Cases* (largely erasing the Privileges and Immunities Clause of the Fourteenth Amendment), *United States v. Cruikshank* (invalidating the convictions of white supremacists prosecuted for murdering black political activists), and *The Civil Rights Cases* (invalidating the public accommodations section of the Civil Rights Act of 1875). According to Gressman, these Justices engineered a "judicial coup d'etat." "Soon," he concluded, "the bold motives and the brave argument of the architects of the constitutional revolution in civil rights were forgotten under the din of a judicial rewriting of their efforts."

I applaud the sentiments that animate Gressman and like-minded critics of the Waite Court. They censure the Justices because of their outrage at the egregious racial oppression that marked the post-Reconstruction era, injustices that were facilitated by the Court's decisions. By ruling as it did in *Cruikshank* and related cases, the Court made federal prosecutions of violent white supremacists considerably more difficult to sustain. By ruling as it did in *The Civil Rights Cases*, the Court condemned southern blacks to a social life hemmed in by private racial oppression. Commentators have railed against the Waite Court, accusing it of apostasy as part of a strategy to persuade Justices and the rest of American society to embrace what they see as the true meaning of the Reconstruction Amendments.

There are several problems with this perspective as it is conventionally articulated. It oversimplifies by exaggerating the extent to which the Waite Court hobbled federal efforts to protect blacks and neglecting the extent to which certain Waite Court rulings extended protection to blacks in circumstances that would have plausibly allowed for a different outcome. In an insightful effort to at least partially rehabilitate the reputation of the Waite Court, Michael Les Benedict points out that in *Cruiskshank* (which was written by Chief Justice Waite), the Court invalidated the indictments on which the prosecutions were based but left unimpaired most of the underlying statutory authority from which subsequent prosecutions could have been launched had there existed in the executive branch the political will to do so. Similarly, Earl M. Maltz is right to insist that *Strauder v. West Virginia*—the first Supreme Court decision interpreting the Fourteenth Amendment in a race relations context—could have come out very differently than it did. Instead of ruling

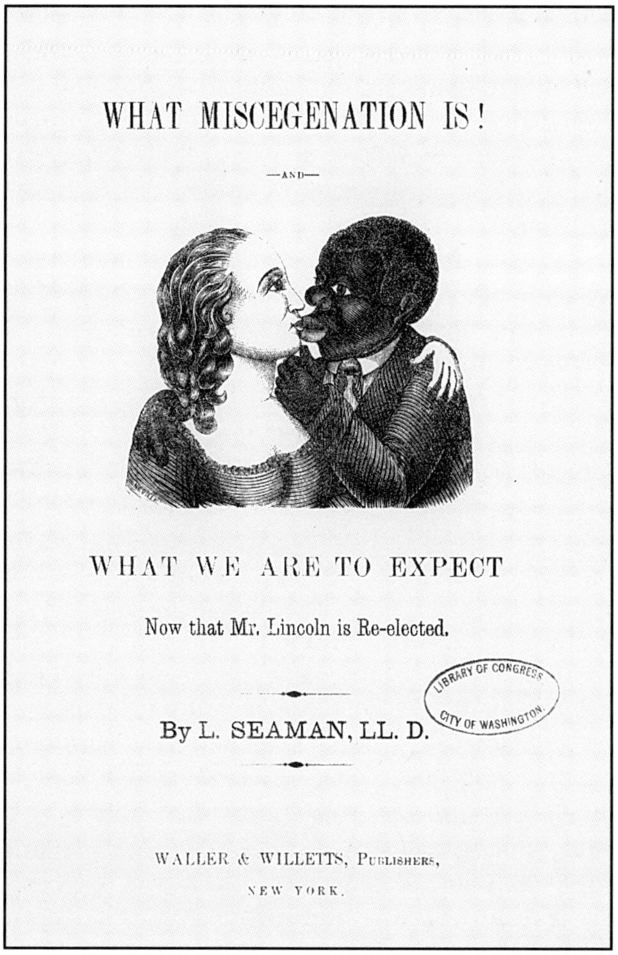

Opponents of the Reconstruction Amendments and of civil rights for African-Americans often brought the specter of miscegenation into the proceedings.

that the Fourteenth Amendment prohibited states from excluding blacks from juries, the Court could have held (as did Justices Nathan Clifford and Stephen J. Field in dissent) that, as originally intended, the Fourteenth Amendment applied only to civil rights and not to political rights such as jury service.

Another way in which the conventional critique of the Waite Court oversimplifies is by exaggerating both the clarity and the grandeur of the Reconstruction Amendments. Although critics of the Waite Court claim that it betrayed the promises of Reconstruction, the fact is that some of those putative promises are rather murky. The best and most consequential example is the delphic injunction of the Equal Protection Clause of the Fourteenth Amendment: "No state shall . . . deny to any person the equal protection of the laws." One of the ongoing struggles over the meaning of that phrase centers upon the permissibility of public authorities using racial criteria to allocate burdens and benefits. Abolitionist Wendell Phillips proposed a version of the Fourteenth Amendment that would have clarified the matter. Phillips' proposal prohibited government from making any racial distinctions.[4] Phillips' proposal, however, was rejected. It was rejected because sufficient numbers of influential framers wanted states to be able to draw racial distinctions, including those that oppressively segregated blacks.

Many associate the Supreme Court's validation of racial segregation with *Plessy v. Ferguson*, the 1896 ruling that is the most infamous of the cases decided by the Supreme Court under the Chief Justiceship of Melville Weston Fuller. In *Plessy* the Court upheld the constitutionality of a Louisiana law which directed that whites and people of color be seated in equal but separate railroad cars. Some have used *Plessy* as a negative example against which to brighten the reputation of the Waite Court. The fact is, however, that the basic theory that animated *Plessy* was already present in *Pace v. Alabama*, a Waite era case decided by a unanimous Court in 1882. *Pace* arose from a challenge to a law that punished more harshly interracial fornicators than other fornicators; while Alabama sentenced the former to imprisonment for two to seven years, it sentenced the latter only to a fine of not less than one hundred dollars and imprisonment for not more than six months. Upholding the constitutionality of this law, the Court reasoned that the law did not invidiously discriminate against blacks insofar as the law applied equally to whites as well to blacks. The white member of an interracial union was just as subject to the higher punishment as the black member of such a union.

Was this, too, a betrayal of the Reconstruction Amendments? A response in the affirmative is appropriate only if it is clear that the Reconstruction Amendments were intended to strike down these and other racial distinctions. The history of the framing of those amendments yields no such clarity. Indeed, the record more supports a conclusion that, considered as a whole, the framers of the Reconstruction Amendments did not intend to abolish white supremacist racial distinctions, than a conclusion that they did intend to abolish them.

The central point of revisionists engaged in rehabilitating the reputation of the Waite Court is that far from betraying the political values of the Republicans who fashioned the Reconstruction Amendments, the Waite Court Justices rather faithfully mirrored those values. Like the most influential wing of the Congressional Republican framers, the Waite Court sought to protect blacks within the framework of constitutional modifications that preserved a state-centered nationalism.

The revisionist defense of the Waite Court invites a broader critique than that conventionally made by critics of the Waite Court. It invites a critique of the Republican framers and their handiwork. There is much to criticize. The Republican framers were far more captive to Negrophibic constituents, much less farsighted about the realistic needs of the newly freed slaves, considerably more naive and opportunistic than they are often portrayed. The Reconstruction Amendments, moreover, are hardly the clear, unsullied, pronouncements of freedom and equality that are unequivocally lauded in countless displays of constitutional fetishism. Like the Constitutional provisions of 1787, the provisions of 1865-1870 were the result of fierce struggles and ugly compromises. What became the Thirteenth Amendment did not obtain Congressional approval when it was first voted upon in 1864. President Abraham Lincoln was forced to the edge of legality, if not beyond, to insure its passage. Considerable evidence suggests that Lincoln used secret promises of presidential patronage to obtain the votes of key members of the House of Representatives. And even with Lincoln's strong backing the Thirteenth Amendment passed the House by an exceedingly narrow margin. The Fourteenth Amendment was condemned by Wendell Phillips and other strong friends of the Negro as "a fatal and total surrender" because it not only failed to enfranchise blacks, but implicitly recognized the right of states to restrict the ballot to whites. What Phillips objected to was Section Two of the Fourteenth Amendment which provides for a reduction in representation in proportion to the number of male citizens denied the suffrage. The Fourteenth Amendment, in other words, did not prohibit racial exclusion from the ballot box but simply stipulated that states would pay a political cost for such exclusion. The Fifteenth Amendment finally provided a degree of federal constitutional protection to black voters. But instead of directly enfranchising blacks, the Amendment merely bars states from excluding persons from the franchise on the basis of race—a provision that invites and has attracted all manner of evasion. Noting that the Fifteenth Amendment would not forbid literacy, property, and education tests that could effectively exclude most blacks from the polls without explicit mention of race, Representative Henry Wilson decried its language as "lame and halting."

The point here is not to argue, as some have, that the Reconstruction Amendments changed little for the good. To the contrary, these amendments represent a major step forward in the moral, cultural, political and legal life of the nation. However, they were—they are—flawed. The Waite Court and those that followed surely failed to do all that they might have to redress the Constitution's deficiencies. But in assigning responsibility, it is important to recognize the breadth and the depth of the problem. The judicial interpreters of the Reconstruction Amendments are appropriate targets of criticism. So too, however, are the Founding Fathers of the post Civil War Constitution and the all-important but tremendously deficient amendments they produced.

Endnotes

[1] 109 U.S. 3 (1883).

[2] *Id.* at 26.

[3] 50 ***Mich. L. Rev.*** 1323 (1952).

[4] Phillips' proposed amendment read: No state shall make any distinction in civil rights and privileges among the naturalized citizens of the United States . . . or among persons born on its soil of parents permanently resident there, on account of race, color, or descent." Quoted in Andrew Kull, ***The Color Blind Constitution*** 62 (1992).

Photo Credits

Page 7, Library of Congress, BC2-13016
Pages 9 and 11, Bettmann Archive
Page 13, Library of Congress, LC-USZ62-2044
Page 15, Library of Congress, LC-USZ62-4514
Page 17, Library of Congress, LC-USZ62-16960
Page 18, Bettmann Archive
Page 23, Print Collection, Miriam and Ira P. Wallach Division of Art, Prints, and Photographs. The New York Public Library. Astor, Lenox and Tilden Foundation.
Page 26, *Centienial History of the Supreme Court*
Page 27, Library of Congress, LC-USZ62-5092
Page 30, Illinois State Historical Society
Page 37, Library of Congress, LC-USZ62-39901
Page 38, Collection of the Supreme Court of the United States
Page 41, Library of Congress, LC-UZ62-84560
Page 42, Library of Congress, LC-USZ62-19190
Page 48, St. Louis Mercantile Library
Page 50, Library of Congress, LC-BH-82779
Page 52, National Portrait Gallery, NPG.72.68
Page 54, Library of Congress, LC-USZ62-12938
Page 55, Bettmann Archive
Page 65, Bureau of Engraving and Printing
Page 66, Rhode Island Historical Society
Page 69, National Portrait Gallery, NPG.78.109
Page 71, National Portrait Gallery, NPG.83.230
Page 76, Library of Congress, LC-USZ62-90771
Page 78, The Historical New Orleans Collection
Pages 80 and 82, Collection of the Supreme Court of the United States
Page 83, Library of Congress, LC-BH826-3701
Page 85, Collection of the Supreme Court of the United States
Page 90, Library of Congress, LC-USZ62-62799
Page 93, National Portrait Gallery, NPG.80.95
Page 99, Library of Congress
Page 101, Library of Congress, LC-USZ62-32501

Contributors

Herman Belz is a Professor of History at the University of Maryland. He is the co-author of *The American Constitution* and the author of *Reconstructing the Union: Theory and Policy During the Civil War.*

Michael Les Benedict is professor of history and adjunct professor of law at The Ohio State University. He is most recently the author of *The Blessings of Liberty: A Concise Constitutional History of the United States*. He has published numerous books and articles particularly in the era of the Civil War and Reconstruction.

Harold Hyman is the William P. Hobby Professor of History and Director, Center for the History of Leadership Institutions at Rice University. He is the author of *A More Perfect Union: The Impact of the Civil War and Reconstruction on the Constitution.*

Ludwell H. Johnson, III, is Professor Emeritus of History at William and Mary College and the author of *Red River Campaign: Politics and Cotton in the Civil War* (1958); *Division and Reunion: America, 1848-1877* (1978) and dozens of journal articles.

Randall Kennedy clerked for Justice Thurgood Marshall and is a professor at Harvard Law School. He is the author of *Race Relations Law*.

Larry Kramer clerked for Justice William J. Brennan, Jr., and is a Professor of Law at New York University School of Law. He is a co-author of *Conflict of Laws*. He is currently at work on a book describing the transformation of Federalism in the early years of the Republic.

Earl Maltz is a Distinguished Professor of Law at Rutgers School of Law. He is the author of *Civil Rights, The Constitution and Congress 1863-1869.*

Mark E. Neely, Jr., is the John Francis Bannon Professor of History and American Studies at St. Louis University. He is the author of *The Fate of Liberty: Abraham Lincoln and Civil Liberties*, which was awarded the Pulitzer Prize for History.

Phillip Paludan is a Professor of History at the University of Kansas. He is the author of *A Covenant with Death: The Constitution, Law and Equality in the Civil War Era.*

G. Edward White is the John Barbee Minor Professor of Law and History, a University Professor and E. James Kelly Research Professor at the University of Virginia. He is the author of *The Marshall Court and Cultural Change, 1815-35* and *Justice Oliver Wendell Holmes: Law and the Inner Self.* Professor White clerked for Chief Justice Earl Warren.